THE FICTION OF JOSEF ŠKVORECKÝ

The Fiction of Josef Škvorecký

Paul I. Trensky

Professor of Comparative Literature
Fordham University, New York

Assisted by Michaela Harnick

St. Martin's Press   New York

© Paul I. Trensky 1991

All rights reserved. For information, write:
Scholarly and Reference Division,
St. Martin's Press, Inc., 175 Fifth Avenue,
New York, N.Y. 10010

First published in the United States of America in 1991

Printed in Hong Kong

ISBN 0-312-05336-3

Library of Congress Cataloging-in-Publication Data
Trensky, Paul I.
    The fiction of Josef Škvorecký / Paul I. Trensky; assisted by
Michaela Harnick.
    p.   cm.
    Includes bibliographical references and index.
    ISBN 0-312-05336-3
    1. Škvorecký, Josef—Criticism and interpretation. I. Harnick,
Michaela. II. Title.
PG5038.S527Z89   1991
891.8'635—dc20   90-43356
                                                                    CIP

For William E. Harkins

Contents

Foreword vii

PART I NOVELS

1 The Cowards 1
2 The End of the Nylon Era 19
3 The Tank Corps 23
4 The Lion Cub 32
5 Miracle 43
6 The Swell Season 60
7 The Engineer of Human Souls 63
8 Scherzo Capriccioso 85

PART II SHORT WORKS

9 Short Stories 99
10 Novelle 104
11 Detective and Mystery Stories 118

Notes 126
Selected Bibliography 128
Index 132

Foreword

Before the emergence of modern totalitarian regimes, authors living and writing in exile were rare. True, Ovid was banished from Rome to a distant province and wrote some of his best works there. Comenius fled the oppression of the Habsburg-led Counter-Reformation and spent some of his most creative years wandering in foreign Protestant lands. Hugo, who opposed the Second Empire, was forced to flee at the height of his career and popularity and wrote prodigiously while abroad. During the nineteenth century numerous Russian authors either were forced, or preferred, to live in Western Europe, among them Herzen, Turgenev, and Gogol.

But it was only with the rise of Fascism and Communism that an author living outside his native country became a common phenomenon. The Revolution of 1917 drove out of Russia and then the Soviet Union scores of writers, poets, critics and other artists. While many exiled authors ceased to write altogether, others, such as Bunin, Khodasevich, Tsvetaeva, Remizov, and Merezhkovsky continued to publish in their native language because the émigré population was large. The works of some were translated into foreign languages, some of these extensively, and, for example, Bunin, while living in exile, won the Nobel Prize. The luckiest were those who were able to use a foreign language as their new creative medium, among them that linguistic virtuoso, Vladimir Nabokov.

The 1920s and 1930s saw the exodus of authors from Italy, Spain and Germany, as well as from other countries threatened by forms of Fascism: Silone, Guillén, Mann, Brecht, Gombrowicz, Miłosz, Molnár, just to name a few. After World War II, the émigré population began to be enriched by refugee authors from Eastern Europe, whose countries were being, one by one, transformed into Soviet-style totalitarian states. Paradoxically, the post-Stalinist era accelerated the influx of émigré authors, since the Communist régimes preferred to allow prominent dissidents to leave or even to expel them rather than letting them be turned into martyrs. The post-war wave brought to the West some of Eastern Europe's most gifted men of letters, men like Solzhenitsyn, Brodsky, Dovlatov, Sinyavsky, Aksyonov or Kosinski.

In comparison with other European countries whose fate is tied to the history of Nazism and Communism, until the 1970s and 1980s

Czechoslovakia produced a relatively small number of exiled authors. A large-scale departure of the intelligentsia is usually prompted by internal developments rather than by external forces, and the German annexation of Bohemia and Moravia in 1939 was too sudden to enable many Czechs to leave. Furthermore, the Munich Agreement also raised the question whether there was a respectable place for them to leave for. The sparse emigration from Czechoslovakia after the Communist takeover in 1948 has a more complex origin. No doubt the physical difficulty of departure played a role, but even more important was the fact that, in contrast to many authors in other East European countries, many Czech authors had traditionally held strong leftist sympathies. Some prominent men of letters in fact welcomed the 1948 coup, and only gradually came to realise that their hopes for a better society through the application of Marxist doctrines had been a mistake.

In the mid-1950s many Czech writers began to assume a progressively greater reformist, liberal, anti-totalitarian stand, a trend which culminated in the late 1960s. In 1968 the vast majority of the Czech intelligentsia supported the Dubček reforms, and a good case could be made for the assertion that without the determined effort on the part of the Czech Writers' Union, the 'Prague Spring' would not have taken place at all, or at least would not have initiated such extensive reforms as it did.

The swing of the Czech intelligentsia away from Marxist dogma did not escape the attention of Moscow, and after the intervention of 1968, the Prague puppet government took special care not to allow Czech writers to assume their traditional political influence. The suppression of freedom of expression was gradual but thorough. Within three years after the demise of the Prague Spring and Dubček's removal, Czechoslovakia was turned into the most repressive country in the East as far as cultural affairs were concerned, and remained so for over two decades.

After 1968, like the Soviet government of the Brezhnev years, the government in Prague generally became satisfied with merely silencing authors, rather than persecuting them physically. Show trials were few in number compared with the Stalinist years, and sentences were relatively restrained. There have been some notable exceptions. The case of the playwright Václav Havel, who spent long periods in jail, is the best known, but he is by no means the only individual who has been singled out for specially harsh treatment. Some authors were voluntarily or involuntarily banished. The list includes some of

Foreword

the most talented contemporary Czech prose writers, playwrights and poets, among them Jiří Grůša, Martin Harníček, Ivan Klíma, Pavel Kohout, Milan Kundera, Arnošt Lustig and Josef Škvorecký. Some of them have fallen silent or almost silent in exile while others continued to write, although primarily for their émigré compatriots. A few of them have been translated into foreign languages.

Among the Czech émigré writers extensively translated into foreign languages, and who have received the greatest critical and popular attention in the West, Milan Kundera and Josef Škvorecký stand out. Whereas the biographies and art of these two writers have much in common, they also differ in many respects, and the search for parallels and contrasts has become a favourite preoccupation of the informed reader, particularly in the émigré community. Since such a comparison does indeed help towards an understanding of Škvorecký's work, I shall not forego the opportunity to make such a comparison, at least in general terms. The works of both authors go well beyond purely national concerns, yet their work is difficult to imagine without the specific historical consciousness of this small country in central Europe. Their 'Czechness' is an integral part of their fiction, and is to a substantial degree responsible for their special appeal, as much as is, say, the 'Russianness' of the works of Solzhenitsyn, or the 'Polishness' of Kosinski. Kundera and Škvorecký are contemporaries, and their moral awareness was shaped by the six-year German occupation, but only for the five-years older Škvorecký did the war years become an inexhaustible source of tales based on memory. While both were born into middle-class families, Kundera, after the war, became a card-carrying Communist, and only after the fall of the Stalin myth did he begin to break with the dogma. Škvorecký, in contrast, always belonged to the opposition. Paradoxically, this circumstance makes Kundera's portrayal of the Czech postwar historical experience incline to the tragic, while Škvorecký's inclines more to the satirical. Kundera's works are never free of the sense of guilt typical of a disenchanted believer, while Škvorecký's openly bristle with an I-told-you-so attitude. Škvorecký, however, carries ideological baggage of his own – namely, his Roman Catholic background. The coming to terms with his religious heritage is one of his works' constants, although it occurs more on the cultural and psychological levels than on the metaphysical, and is mostly treated with a good deal of irony. The works of both are never devoid of hope for a better future for their country, even when the authors sometimes appear to argue the opposite. Still, Škvorecký is by temperament an eternal optimist despite his frequent use of a melancholy mask.

While the work of both manifests intense historical consciousness, the innermost selves of both authors are non-political. Kundera called himself 'a hedonist trapped in a world politicised in the extreme', and the same, and perhaps even more so, applies to Škvorecký. Their sensuality is revealed in their preoccupation with sexuality, but even here significant differences can be observed. Kundera is an inventor of surprisingly intricate, exquisite and novel sexual situations with a flavour of decadence. Škvorecký depicts a much simpler, rudimentary, occasionally crude, but never vulgar, basically passionless, sexuality. While both Kundera and Škvorecký (despite their initial political differences) develop their art within the West European cultural context, each of them draws on a different tradition. Kundera is an intellectual writer *par excellence*, who was, first of all, influenced by French culture, with its ideal of well-made, cerebral art (his declared love is the age of the Enlightenment), and second, by the central-European philosophical novel. In contrast, Škvorecký's foreign models are English and American literature, from Swift to Hemingway, Faulkner, Dos Passos, Graham Greene, and Raymond Chandler. Kundera's writing is most powerful when blending action with thought, fiction with essay, while the ideological passages in Škvorecký's works generally diminish their effectiveness. Škvorecký has an irreverent attitude towards closed structures in his philosophy as well as his aesthetics. His most successful form is an open-ended, improvisational, first-person narrative. It is not by accident that his work has been compared to the jazz form, while Kundera likes to relate his work to classical music. As a stylist, Škvorecký is by far the more accomplished of the two. He is a true virtuoso of modern Czech, whose literary potential he has significantly expanded, in both narrative and dialogue. In comparison with Škvorecký, Kundera's prose is dry and two-dimensional. It is precisely for this reason that Škvorecký's work loses much of its flavour when rendered into another language, and in spite of his success in the English-speaking world during the past decade, his Anglo-American translators have thus far somewhat failed him.

Škvorecký has sometimes been accused of a lack of discipline, and even of displaying empty frivolity. However, this type of criticism is based on a misunderstanding of the specific nature of Škvorecký's creative temperament. If he is frivolous, it is a studied frivolity, one that, far from reflecting a superficial approach to life, constitutes a conscious reaction to the historical experience of his generation, an experience replete with crippling, artificial ideological constructs. Like Hašek (or, in a different way, Karel Čapek), Škvorecký believes that some of life's greatest wisdom is rooted in the frivolous and the ordinary, and his characters and situations, as well as the structural design of his works, reflect this attitude. His narratives twist and turn, accelerate and decelerate, digress, surprise, and on occasion disturb or annoy, especially lovers of clear and pure form.

Škvorecký's writing career spans about four decades. He has been a productive, but not a prodigiously prolific writer, in spite of the fact that he has a distinctly 'easy-pen' temperament. No doubt political circumstances have considerably dampened his creativity. Up to the time of his emigration in 1968, he could never be certain whether any of his works would be published, and he wrote primarily 'for the drawer'. For example, his first published novel, *The Cowards*, was completed in 1949, yet it was not published until nine years later; *The Tank Corps* was started by 1952, but was to be published only in 1969. Moreover, the reception of his published works was closely related to the ebbs and flows of liberalisation in Czechoslovakia. Such a situation is hardly conducive to long-term creative plans; furthermore, during the Stalinist years, samizdat writing and the circulation of manuscripts was a life-threatening proposition. Much of Škvorecký's literary activity in the 1950s and 1960s was limited to translations of British and American authors. In addition, according to Škvorecký, four of his books (three murder mysteries and an adventure story for children) were published under friends' names in the 1960s; he has to this day steadfastly refused publicly to identify them.

After his emigration, Škvorecký, aided by his wife Zdena Salivarová, a respected author in her own right, conceived the idea of launching their own publishing house. Sixty-Eight Publishers, while originally intended as an outlet for his own works, became in the 1970s and 1980s the leading publishing house of Czech literature in the West. While the Toronto-based Sixty-Eight Publishers eliminated the problem of publication of Škvorecký's work in Czech, there has been a continued substantial delay in the publication of Škvorecký's work in translation, especially in English. For example, *The Engineer of Human Souls*, internationally his most successful novel, appeared in English only in 1984, seven years after its publication in Czech.

This is in spite of the fact that he is viewed in Canada, where he now has made his home, as a Canadian author, and receives Canadian literary awards. Škvorecký has been active in various genres. He has written poetry, a play, filmscripts, literary and film criticism. His principal medium, fiction, consists of novels, novelle, short stories, and detective fiction. The centre of gravity of his writing lies in the 'big' genre, the novel. The most important novels are *The Cowards* (1958), *Miracle* (1972), and *The Engineer of Human Souls* (1977). These three works may be regarded as a loosely conceived triptych, from both a structural and a thematic point of view. All three contain an extensive historico-autobiographical element, and are first-person narratives related by the author's autobiographical surrogate, Danny Smiřický. This character, together with other devices, serves to establish a sense of continuity between the three works, however great the difference in the times of their origin and the periods covered in each. The fictionalised autobiographical element is also present in other works by Škvorecký, notably in *The Tank Corps* (1954, published 1969) and *The Lion Cub* (1967). However, the narrative focus and point of view are somewhat different in these two works. While *The Tank Corps* features Danny Smiřický, the work is not actually narrated by him and there is in fact little interest in Smiřický as a character. *The Lion Cub* features an altogether different narrator, but nevertheless it is replete with episodes derived from Škvorecký's own experience. But the important aspect of the autobiographical triptych, extensive episodes from the author's narrative surrogate's youth, is absent. Škvorecký's fifth major novel, *Scherzo Capriccioso* (1980), constitutes a decisive break from the autobiographical (or more accurately, pseudo-autobiographical) mode, being a fictionalised account of the life and times of the composer Antonín Dvořák, narrated predominantly from the omniscient author narrative viewpoint. However, Škvorecký employs here the same cut-and-paste technique found in his other major post-exile novels.

In view of the overlapping structures and themes of Škvorecký's fiction, and in view of the absence of other systematic studies of the author's work, I have decided for the purpose of this book to use the simplest approach possible. I have organised the material as an extended critical guide, using a genre-by-genre discussion in a straight chronological order. Accordingly, I have divided the book into two major parts. The first part deals with his major as well as his minor novels: *The Cowards*, *The End of the Nylon Era*, *The Tank Corps*, *The Lion Cub*, *Miracle*, *The Engineer of Human Souls*, *The Swell Season*, and *Scherzo Capriccioso*. The second part is divided into three sections. The first deals with Škvorecký's short stories; the second deals with his three novellas, *The Emöke Legend*, *The Bass Saxophone*, and *The End of a Parish Priest*; and the third is an overview of his 'sidekick' fiction, detective stories and mysteries. Due to the considerable time lag between the works' origins and the times of their publication, within each section the discussion follows the time of origin. Quotations from Škvorecký's works not yet published in English are in my own translation. As regards quotations from works available in English, in view of the fact that the quality of the translations varies, in some instances I have used the translated editions; in others I have used my own translations.

Most of this monograph was written in the mid-1980s and completed months before the 'velvet' revolution of November 1989. Škvorecký is no longer banned in his native country and after twenty years his works are again being published there. The interest in Škvorecký, the symbol of political resistance, will now decisively shift towards Škvorecký, the author. It is my belief that the new situation will lead to the general understanding that he is one of the great Czech prose writers of this century.

Part I
Novels

1 The Cowards

The Cowards (*Zbabělci*) was written in 1948–49 when Škvorecký was twenty-four years old. However, since by then Socialist Realist dogma had begun to be enforced, its publication was unthinkable. It was not until 1958, when the Thaw was fully underway, that its first publication took place. Even then, however, its appearance proved premature. The conservative wing of the Party was ready for a counteroffensive, and so it used *The Cowards* as one of its principal arguments against liberalisation. The book was banned in short order, and Škvorecký was severely reprimanded. Those responsible for the publication were demoted or dismissed from their positions. The novel was republished in 1964, in an already substantially changed cultural climate, and was greeted almost universally as a major work of post-war Czech prose.

The action of *The Cowards* is set in a small town in northern Bohemia called Kostelec (a fictitious name Škvorecký uses for his native town, Náchod, in all his works). The period covered is the last few days of the German occupation of Bohemia and Moravia, from 4 May through 11 May, 1945. The novel is written in the form of a loosely structured diary kept by the twenty-year-old Danny Smiřický (the author's autobiographical surrogate), the son of upper-middle-class parents. After he graduates from high school, he has to work as a labourer in the local Messerschmidt fighter-plane factory. Descriptive passages are intertwined with passages that are confessional or meditative in nature, as well as with situations in which Danny almost always participates. Each of the eight chapters covers the events of one day. They are uneven in length: the longest fills 85 pages, and the shortest a mere four. Most chapters begin with Danny leaving home and end with his return; the exceptions are chapter 1, which starts *in medias res*, and chapter 4, in which the narrator does not leave his home at all because he has contracted a brief illness.

The Cowards is not an historical novel, since its main focus is upon fictional characters, in particular upon the inner life of the narrator. The historical setting, however, is important, not only because of the influence events have upon the principal character, but also because they dictate the very structure of the novel. Danny is cast in the role of the chronicler of situations into which he is sometimes voluntarily, and sometimes accidentally, drawn. The action is fragmentary, and other characters are not developed to any extensive degree. Numerous individuals appear and disappear, with only the consciousness of the narrator tying events together. Besides the protagonist, only one other character stands out significantly: the local belle, Irena, the elusive object of Danny's persistent wooing. However, even she comes alive more through Danny's fantasies than through the action.

The historical background of the novel is formed by the isolated uprisings of the Czechs against the Germans during the final days of the occupation, which, for patriotic reasons, came to be called, with a good deal of exaggeration, the National Revolution. From a military point of view, the uprisings were of little importance. They took place several days after Hitler's death, when the surrender of the Germans was a foregone conclusion. That the uprisings led to some fierce fighting, especially in Prague, stemmed mainly from the fact that the activities of the insurgents were hindering the retreat of the German armies from the Eastern Front to the West. The objective of the troops was to surrender to the Allies rather than to the Russians, and much of their escape route happened to lead through Bohemia. In some parts of the country, military activities lasted until two days after the official surrender of the German Army. The myth of the 'revolution' was fostered after the war to help the Czechs regain national self-esteem, but gradually it acquired more political overtones. In disregard of historical facts, Communist propagandists began to interpret the revolution as a part of the general struggle of the proletariat against capitalism as epitomised by the Nazi regime. The dramatisation of the idea became particularly common after the Communist takeover in 1948, when numerous historical studies as well as novels and films on the 'revolution' appeared.

The novelty of *The Cowards* was that it did not portray the 'revolution' from the customary elevated ideological point of view, but from the 'low' perspective of an ordinary individual. This ideologically untarnished account provided a new insight into the 'revolution'. Stripped of its elaborate ideological interpretations, the 'revolution' appeared to be more an amalgam of calculated, self-serving acts by opportunists, careerists, and frenzied, sometimes self-destructive, hotheads. Heroism, although not absent in the novel, proves to be a rather elusive concept, while cowardice, vindictiveness, and brutality are much more clearly discernible. An underlying feeling of absurdity emerges from the description of the 'revolution', a feeling that eventually transcends its narrow significance and becomes a condemnation of wars and violence in general.

One important meaning of the novel is the quest for authentic experience, a quest that lies outside political concerns.

The paradox of the novel is that while its main emotional and ideational thrust lies beyond topical considerations, it owes much of its effect to its specific historical setting. In spite of the fact that the novel is not overtly polemical, it manages to be iconoclastic towards the 'revolution'. The devices employed to this end are various: the very account of the events is organised in such a way as to create the impression of purposelessness. From the very first day of the narrative, the Czechs are hopelessly divided into at least three factions. The strongest faction consists of representatives of the old, pre-war establishment, who belong predominantly to the upper middle class. They want to proceed as cautiously as possible, their objective being a negotiated 'revolution' without risk. Another faction is made up of those vaguely identified with the Communists, whose plans are more radical. Finally, there are a number of individuals of anarchist disposition who want the 'revolution' to go their way.

As the Germans move through the town, the behaviour of the population undergoes numerous changes. When it appears that the troops are tired and resigned to being disarmed by the Czechs, the streets overflow with revolutionary enthusiasm. As soon as a handful of German soldiers becomes less tolerant, the patriots retreat quickly into hiding. The confusion increases when thousands of released prisoners of war and former inmates of concentration camps pass through the town.

In spite of the portrayal of individual and collective tragedies, the narrative frequently borders on the satirical and bizarre. Thus the self-styled commander of the town, who was a colonel in the pre-war Czechoslovak Army, suffers a heart-attack when a German fighter plane makes a low-level flight over the town. The first 'combat' takes place not between the Czechs and the Germans, but between members of the two leading factions, in the form of a street brawl that brings in the Germans to restore order. The volunteers, including Danny, are not trained to use weapons, but instead are subjected to ludicrous bureaucratic procedures and drilled in military etiquette. The 'revolution' erupts fully only after the arrival of the Soviet troops, when there is no longer any doubt about the end of German resistance. The 'revolution' manifests itself principally in the local patriots' senseless killing and torture of the remnants of the German Army.

The main device for the downgrading of the ideological significance of the 'revolution' is the narrator's point of view. *The Cowards* is not a typical 'naive-eye' account. The story is coloured by the intellectually sophisticated, albeit emotionally immature, attitudes of the protagonist. The basic standpoint is established from the very first sentence of the novel, when Danny and his friends are discussing the 'revolution' during a rehearsal of their jazz band in a local pub: 'We were sitting over at the Port Arthur and Benno said, "Well,. it looks like the revolution's been postponed for a while." "Yes," I said and stuck the reed in my mouth. "For technical reasons, right?"'[1] (p. 11) The discussion between Danny and his friends on this topic is extensive, but even more important are the internal monologues of Danny: 'But there was supposed to be a revolution. And there had to be one. A lot of people wanted a revolution. A lot of important people, too. And a lot of these had bad records that needed cleaning up fast.' (p. 42) 'I couldn't imagine anybody shooting. The druggist, or Mr. Krocan, who owned a factory? Crazy.' (p. 46)

Besides the direct evaluative comments by the narrator and by his friends, the novel contains extensive descriptive passages which are an indirect denigration of the 'revolution'. One central device is a sort of dramatic tableau created by moving the focus from the general to the particular in a manner reminiscent of a movie-camera technique. The closer the focus, the more senseless the activities appear. Frequently, such description is amplified by grotesque details or by a metaphor. For example, one scene contains a description of an unexpected approach of fresh German troops into Kostelec that touches off a panic among the frenzied citizenry. The description culminates in a simile, comparing the flight of a crippled woman to an athlete performing his gymnastic routine:

> Something was going on. People were milling around on both sides of the church. They were running away from the square behind the church and jamming the streets on either side of the square. Something was going on behind the church but you couldn't see what. Clusters of people had stopped in front of the post office to stare. All I could see was the backs of people's heads, tilted hats, and dishevelled hairdos. Soon it was almost deserted on both sides of the church. I watched Mrs Salačová, the lame seamstress, swinging along fast on her crutches. My curiosity was aroused. From around the left side of the church a soldier emerged with bayonet and the square grew silent. The soldier advanced slowly in

his grey helmet and jackboots, an ominous figure. A second one came out close behind him. Then from behind the other side of the church more soldiers appeared . . . The crowd silently pressed back into the side streets and doorways. Mrs Salačová hurried along frantically on her crutches. I watched her go. Her body swung in frenzied arcs like a pendulum, or as if she were doing calisthenics on the parallel bars. (p. 64)

The use of a physical deformity or of incongruity for the purpose of achieving a grotesque effect can be found in many variations. Thus, when the uprising is finally about to take place, the volunteers assemble in a local brewery (perhaps a deliberate allusion to Hitler's early 'beer putsch'). Some of the volunteers are dressed for this occasion in their ill-fitting pre-war military uniforms, while others wear sportswear of all kinds, including hunting, mountain-climbing and hiking dress. The narrator lays considerable emphasis on their appearance, thus creating an image more reminiscent of a fancy-dress ball than a combat unit. Prominent pieces of various individuals' attire become their trademark, one to accompany them in most subsequent references to them in the novel.

Škvorecký's method is particularly successful in the description of various objects that acquire symbolic connotations. The account of the repeated furling and unfurling of flags and banners during the various phases of the 'revolution' is a good example of the employment of grotesque symbolism through physical deformity:

> At Kaldoun's there was a terribly long flag that hung from the attic window almost all the way to the ground. It was nearly sixty feet long. It was a real monster of a flag . . . Somebody was pulling Kaldoun's flag in through the attic window as fast as he could. It looked as though the dormer window up in the attic was swallowing a long piece of red and white macaroni. (p. 100)

In the following scene, describing the hoisting of the flag over the citadel of the town, Škvorecký uses his technique of contrasting moods, by first allowing the scene to attain an idyllic dimension, then turning the image into sentimental, vulgar kitsch. The process goes on entirely in the mind of the narrator as he imagines the future bastardisation and commercialisation of the holiday spirit by the employment of traditional, banal iconography:

> I looked up and saw a huge flag majestically fluttering from the turret of the castle. The Czech flag. The sun was shining on it and

the cupola of the castle was bright red; the hill on which the castle stood was bright with lilacs in bloom. It was like a picture on a candy box. An extremely patriotic picture. A picture to remember. It would certainly inspire Mr Leitner to paint it, working in a bunch of people in Sokol [Czech patriotic gymnastics association] dress and the little girls in old-fashioned peasant costumes, and over in one corner, [the historical novelist] Alois Jirásek. No. Alois Jirásek in one corner, and Božena Němcová [village novelist from the National Revival] in another. President Masaryk in the upper left hand corner, President Beneš in the right and at the bottom Alois Jirásek and Božena Němcová. And then he would display it in his shop window. (p. 56)

The main satirical thrust of the novel is directed against the middle classes, to which Danny himself belongs, but whose values he refuses to accept. The activities of the working class, generally identified as the Communists, are described only sketchily. In spite of the fact that Danny participates in a clash between his 'legitimate' patrol and a group of vigilantes deemed to be the Communists, there is no apparent hostility in their portrayal. Unlike the members of his own class, who are individualised, the Communists are anonymous figures generally referred to as 'chlapi' (real men) who inspire both respect and unease in Danny. They are instinctively perceived by him as a more robust, elemental force than the class to which he himself belongs. However, their objectives are seen as being just as senseless as those of the moderate faction. A similar observation can be made about the Soviet Army that finally marches in and repels the Germans. Danny is overwhelmed by the appearance of the ungroomed, rather undisciplined masses of soldiers with predominantly Asiatic features. But at the same time he keenly feels their vitality. He recalls the poem by Aleksander Blok, 'The Scythians', in which the Russian poet presents a vision of the elemental forces of the East sweeping away overcivilised and feeble Western society:

> The air was filled with creaks and rattles and the crack of the long whips. Like a wild stampede, they rumbled past in rapid procession – the red-cheeked Russians towering over the rumps of their flea-bitten ponies bellowing out their Russian songs. The people on the sidewalks gawked. The wagons hurtled by at breakneck speed, the wiry little horses tossing their manes. There was an endless line of them. Their smell filled the air. The smell of tundra or taiga – and, breathing it in and looking at those weatherbeaten men's

faces, it seemed incredible that such people really existed, people who knew nothing about jazz or girls either, probably, and who just shot by – unshaven, revolvers strapped around their greasy pants, bottles of vodka stuck in their hip pockets, excited, drunk, and triumphant, not thinking about things I thought about, completely different from me, and awfully strange, yet with something awfully attractive about them, too. (p. 392)

The tone changes quickly, however, when the narrative turns to the description of the Soviet military establishment. The victory celebration at which official representatives of the local revolutionaries and high-ranking officials of the Red Army deliver thundering orations to the assembled citizenry of Kostelec forms one of the strongest passages of satirical prose in the novel. Once again, the device of bizarre physical incongruity is applied – the principal speaker, a Soviet general, is described as a 'ruddy-faced fatso, wearing red riding breeches with double stripes down the sides and a chestful of medals'. (p. 395) The scene is given a particularly grotesque dimension when the assembled citizens have to listen to the playing of not only the Soviet and Czechoslovak national anthems, but also those of two other great-power allies, the French and the British. The scene is reminiscent of a passage in *Animal Farm*.

In spite of the fact that the action revolves around the conflict between the Czechs and Germans, on the ideological level the generation conflict occupies a significantly more important place. The negative attitude of Danny and his friends towards the 'revolution' is soon understood as part of their dislike of traditional values. Danny and the other young people are in search of a worthy ideal, and they instinctively understand that the 'revolution' in its official form will not bring new values but restore old ones which they distrust. Their conception of a revolution is anarchistic and ecstatic. It contrasts with the orderly objectives of the revolutionary establishment. The contrasting conceptions, first of revolution as a means of bringing in the new, then that of restoring or preserving the old, occurs again and again. Thus when the radio reports that Prague Castle is on fire, Danny's father clenches his fist in anger and despair while deep in his heart Danny feels satisfaction at the news; it awakens in him the vision of a new and better world that will rise from the ruins. The strange inconsistency in the behaviour of Danny and the other young men is attributable to their ambivalent perception of the historical situation and the values of their fathers. On the one hand, they repeatedly express their contempt for the uprising, but, on the other, they are prone to occasional outbursts of impulsive, reckless, almost self-destructive courage. While the conflict between the Czech nationalists and the German occupation forces leads to a clear resolution, the generation conflict survives the events – indeed, the gap between the old and the young becomes greatly magnified by the Allies' victory.

The motif of the 'revolution' is not the only one to dramatise the generation conflict. The second, and in many ways more important, motif is that of jazz, a motif that pervades the novel. The narrative begins with a rehearsal of the jazz band of which Danny is a member and ends with the description of a public concert by the band. Jazz occupies an important place in Danny's interior monologue, emerging sometimes in the most surprising circumstances.

Jazz, like other leading motifs of the novel, has a multiple significance on various narrative levels. Jazz is not merely a musical form, but rather a world-view. This point requires clarification for a reader unfamiliar with the history of jazz in Europe. Most European countries became acquainted with the various forms of jazz during the 1920s and 1930s, but it received little recognition as an art form. While the broad public was interested more in the watered-down version of jazz played by many European dance bands, only the youngest generation, and only a small segment of this generation, developed a passionate thirst for genuine jazz. The cult of jazz spread principally among young people from the upper-middle and upper classes. In Nazi Germany and in countries occupied by the Germans, recordings of leading black jazz bands were available even during the first two years of the war, despite the official condemnation of jazz as the product of an inferior race. After 1941, when Hitler declared war on the United States, the importation of jazz recordings ceased. They became collectors' items and reached astronomical prices on the underground market. A new wave of jazz reached Europe in the final year of the war with the American Forces broadcasting stations. By then jazz had reached the proportions of a religious cult among the young, and local bands imitating American models mushroomed. The fact that jazz was the product of American culture gave the cult a certain symbolic dimension as a form of anti-Nazi resistance. To some degree, it also became a part of the idolisation of America as a utopian land of freedom and full, uninhibited, adventurous life. The older generation had little appreciation of jazz and sided in this respect with the official line.

In Eastern Europe after World War II the Communist ideologues were faced with a dilemma in regard to jazz. On the one hand, they were well aware of the pro-Western disposition of jazz enthusiasts, but, on the other, they found it difficult to condemn jazz, a product of the 'oppressed' black race in whom they saw a natural ally, especially in what are now called Third-World countries. At first there was an attempt to draw a line between genuine jazz and its commercial by-products. However, this dual approach proved impractical during the intensification of the Cold War, which required simplified distinctions. Therefore jazz fell into total disfavour with the Communist ideologists, and was treated even more harshly by the Communist than by the Nazi authorities.

The idolisation of jazz in *The Cowards* ought to be viewed not merely as a reconstruction of the war era, but also in part as reflecting the reaction against the repression of jazz by the Communist government after the war. This double significance gave the work, on its first appearance, a special meaning. Indeed, the suggestion that jazz was meant as an expression of anti-German sentiment is virtually absent in the novel (although this aspect is apparent in some later works by Škvorecký that are also set in the war). In *The Cowards* jazz is treated as a phenomenon standing outside historical problems. In Danny's mind jazz possesses a significance clearly superior to that of the revolutionary events around him. It is a quintessential metaphor of a free, uninhibited life. Danny's participation in the world of jazz takes place on several levels. On the factual level the narrative deals extensively with his band's rehearsals and concerts, as well as with his listening to recorded or broadcast music. Information about the composition and music of this band is sketchy and contradictory. It purports to be a Dixieland-type ensemble headed by the piano player Fonda. Those who search for autobiographical clues in Škvorecký's novels should view this group more as a dream band of the author than as an accurate account of his musical activity during that period. While Škvorecký was, like Danny, a saxophone player, photographs of Škvorecký's band, published later on, show a much more conventional ensemble resembling a typical dance band of the time. In his autobiographical *Self-Dig-Book: A Personal Festschrift* the author claims that the band in which he played was a sixteen-piece 'big band' and that he reduced the number to a Dixieland size for the sake of narrative economy.[2] Even then, not all players are treated by the narrator with equal attention: some are developed more extensively, while others are only mentioned by name.

Jazz is repeatedly used as the demarcation line between generations in *The Cowards*. 'Some old geezer stood planted in the doorway with half a pint of beer in his hand, staring at us', the narrator says in describing a confrontation between the generations during one of the band's rehearsals. 'I could read his mind. His eyes looked like two bugles and he had a mouth like a tuba. He certainly didn't think the stuff we were producing was music. We didn't either, really. Not just music. For us it was something like the world. Like before Christ and after Christ.' (p. 30) Even Danny's father, who is otherwise portrayed as an attractive character, does not escape the stigma of ignorance because of his lack of appreciation of jazz.

The motif of jazz is an important conduit for the description of the inner life of the protagonist. To Danny jazz is a bridge to the world of the imagination, its function analogous to that of hallucinogenic drugs. It is an intensifier of sensual perception, facilitating a trip to levels where dream and reality merge. Jazz is conceived of romantically as an experience beyond intellectual limitations. It is a promise of a life without the need of a search for its meaning. The sensuality of the experience of jazz is underscored by the repeated intermingling of this motif with that of sex. Danny's saxophone carries strikingly Freudian associations. 'The bamboo reed tasted good as it always did. One of the reasons I liked to play tenor was because I liked to suck on the reed.' (p. 11) 'The saxophone, the sexiest instrument there is. Sexophone. A real honey-pot for girls.' (p. 86) The instrument thus becomes a link between his infancy (the oral stage), and his manhood (the phallic implications of the instrument). The idolatry of the instrument also has some masturbatory connotations. 'I thought about Irena and about how happy I'd been yesterday, but happiness had vanished and would never return, and then I put my hand on my saxophone case and thought to myself, I love it – that live, silver, comforting thing lying in that case.' (p. 409) 'I was sucking on the tenor reed and fiddling with the valves on its nice, cool, metallic body.' (p. 287)

The saxophone as the symbol of sexual prowess occurs in almost all Danny's narcissistic fantasies, whether they are related to present or past events, or to his utopian future filled with dreamgirls. 'I got up and Mr Flux turned the spotlight on me and there I stood, all in white, with my sideburns and glistening saxophone and Irena was down there in the darkened ballroom watching ... And when I thought of the future, I could see notes in front of me on a music stand and a band up on the stage and me with a golden saxophone and beautiful girls wearing low-cut gowns and a lost look in their eyes from the music and smiles on their lips when I looked their way.' (p. 200)

Danny Smiřický, the narrator, is the dominant figure in the novel. We never cease to focus our attention on him, no matter how dramatic the events surrounding him may be. George Gibian has found only three analogues in world literature to this feature in the novel – Raskolnikov, Stephen Dedalus and Holden Caulfied.[3] Danny is a character who eludes classification from an historical, literary or psychological point of view. During the time when Škvorecký was in official disgrace, establishment critics found Danny decadent, reactionary, cynical and even satanic. By the same token, however, he could be called politically progressive, idealistic, outgoing and honest. During the time of Škvorecký's rehabilitation in the 1960s, his apologists emphasised the multifarious aspects of his nature. Milan Jungman, the principal critic of *Literární noviny* (Literary News), the official organ of the Czechoslovak Writers' Union, wrote:

> Some people were satisfied with quoting some of Danny's thoughts and by so doing they believed that they had characterized him, placed him, and defined him. But no quotation, no characterization, could encompass Danny in his entirety, without qualification, in his full value as the author created him . . . It was always possible to use one quotation to negate another, one characterization to negate another. Danny is made up of numerous contradictory features which, combined, form an indivisible whole.[4]

Virtually the entire image of Danny is derived from his own narrative. The information obtained about him from the responses of other people is negligible, and even when we have such responses, they are coloured by his own attitudes to them. From the point of view of cultural history, the character's image was influenced to some degree by the post-war proliferation of existential heroes (or anti-heroes). The four-year gap between the events described in the novel and the time of the novels' genesis played an important role in the shaping of the character. Škvorecký's work reflects the atmosphere of the late 1940s as much as – and perhaps even more than – that of the end of World War II. Danny's slightly anachronistic traits were probably responsible for some of the misunderstandings that arose when the book was first published in 1958. The feeling of alienation that pervades Danny's interior monologue was essentially atypical of a young man at the end of World War II. Another difficulty which the establishment critics had with the character was that he did not undergo any significant development in the novel, as required by the tenets of Socialist Realism. *The Cowards* is indeed far from being a *Bildungsroman*. Danny's basic psychological disposition consists of a blend of juvenile romantic escapism and painfully self-conscious scepticism, traits which are as pronounced at the beginning of the novel as at the end.

As we observed, Danny's own alienation is perceived by himself as an historical and social fact. He understands that he is a member of a class which has lost its vitality and that will probably not regain the dominant role which it enjoyed before the War. The clumsily manipulated 'revolution' was perhaps its final show of power. The generation conflict in the novel is closely related to this particular discovery. However, Danny's alienation goes deeper than that of his friends of the same age and social class. They all seem to have some kind of identity, no matter how limited. Beno is content in his role of henpecked lover; Rosťa is unshakeable in his affection for the whorish Dagmar; Zdeněk is complacent in the one-dimensional life-style of an athlete, while Fonda is not only a competent leader of the jazz band, but also has clear, 'respectable' plans for his future. The language of symbols is clear in his portrayal: he wants to become an architect. Danny, in contrast, with the exception of his immersion in jazz, has no firm beliefs or serious pursuits, and his plans for the future are daydreams about more jazz and love affairs.

Danny suffers from a pronounced sense of emotional inadequacy. He suffers from an acute awareness of his inability to find fulfilment because of his analytical, sceptical nature, which deprives him of spontaneity. This feeling asserts itself in a variety of situations. In the erotic sphere, his inability to be carried away is expressed as follows:

> Then I started thinking about Beno. It was funny, I knew, but this was something I couldn't, and probably never would understand. Allowing yourself to be roped up and led around and humiliated like that, losing control over yourself that way. I've never lost control of myself. I could never get so mad at anybody that I'd really blow my top. And love never made me lose my head either. When I had my arms around some girl and was jabbering away, I had to act as though I was talking like that out of sheer ecstasy and excitement and all that kind of thing. I really could have talked pretty sensibly, only that probably would have made her mad, and so I'd always talked a lot of nonsense. I had to act like I was

completely gone on her and that she took my breath away and so on, and, at the same time, I always had an embarrassing feeling that girls could see right through my act and that they were laughing at me. But none of them really saw through it. (p. 23)

The sense of alienation is experienced by Danny not merely in intimate situations, but even more strongly when he is surrounded by the masses. The experience of being swept away by identification with the masses is entirely foreign to him. During the victory celebration, which is a pandemonium of people of all ages, nationalities, and races, Danny continuously feels his aloneness:

The Frenchmen whirled the girls around the floor till their skirts flew up and you could see their silly pink panties and when the song was over, one of the dancing Frenchmen yelled at me, 'Vive la France! Vive les Soviets! Vive la paix!' and he smiled. I smiled back at him and wanted to yell something too, but suddenly, I was embarrassed. I would have liked to holler something back but I couldn't. The best I could come up with was a grin and I waved my hand and was furious that I did not know how to shout like that and it ruined the music for me. . . . I couldn't bring myself to do it, I was not spontaneous enough. (p. 238)

Sometimes the depressive mood is overcome by a pose of superiority when Danny persuades himself that spontaneity is a sign of intellectual limitations: 'I felt mad at the Frenchman, that damn fool. Why should I holla just because he had? I was glad that the Protectorate was over but I didn't feel any urge to go crazy just because of that. And I could not stand the feeling that somebody was standing there just waiting for me to go crazy'. (p. 238)

More often the bitter taste of emotional displacement is unremitting. During the last three days of the narrative, Danny befriends a group of British soldiers who have spent five years as prisoners of war in a German camp. The relationship has all the signs of sincerity and spontaneity; however, during the parting scene, Danny is overcome by an acute feeling of disillusion, caused not so much by the soldiers' departure as by the sudden realisation that the brief friendship had been self-delusion, a mirage created by his ability to communicate in English and by his associations with Anglo-American prewar movies. 'I knew my world was leaving along with them but I wasn't sure whether it had ever really been my world at all, whether it hadn't been just a world which I'd known only from the movies, that the only thing I really had in common with them was the English language . . . It was all a big act.' (p. 405)

The depressive tendency, however, occupies only a part, and not even the larger part, of Danny. The other part of his personality is optimistic and often even wildly aggressive. Danny is one of the first of the Czechs in Kostelec to revolt openly against the German soldiers and during the climactic hours of the 'revolution' he is involved in one of its most dangerous actions. On occasion, he exhibits a remarkable ability to overcome emotional crises, sometimes by using naive but effective sophistry in his interior monologues, sometimes by finding sensuous stimuli and sometimes by shifting his attention to transcendental or quasi-transcendental ideals. Instructive in this respect is his love for Irena. Throughout the novel he feels that he has little chance of winning her, because of her loyalty to her insipid boyfriend. Yet he pursues her with an almost comic obsession, despite the fact that at the bottom of his heart he is well aware that Irena is a girl of ordinary intelligence and rather bland beauty. His feelings oscillate between genuine love for her and a sober view that she is 'a stupid girl'. He does not hesitate to put aside his heartache and make love to other girls whenever they are available. Ultimately, all of them, including Irena, are in his eyes only temporary substitutes for the true love which he hopes to find in Prague, where he plans to move after the war is over. Prague, where his 'ideal woman' awaits him, where more and better jazz is played, becomes for him a Chekhovian myth of fulfilment.

Despite his moods of depression and sense of loneliness, Danny has an ironical perception of the world and of himself; he also has a keen sense of humour. He has a tendency to minimise his plights rather than to indulge in them, and he even has moments of unreserved, overflowing ecstasy that reach almost metaphysical proportions. 'And when I thought about it honestly, it was a good thing, too, that I was in love with Irena and that she was going with Zdeněk and maybe I was better off just daydreaming and writing testimonials to my love. Of course, it would have been nice, too, if I'd been going with her myself. Everything was nice. Absolutely everything. Actually, there wasn't anything bad in the whole wide world.' (p. 19)

The reason for Danny's depressive stages may be seen in his belief in a hedonistic life-style, but also in his awareness of its limitations. He has a need for transcendental experiences, but, because he is a sceptic, he is unable to find them. Eventually, being young and still largely uncorrupted by the vices of the world, he always returns to his belief in the sensual. There is something engagingly naive in Danny who, in spite of his considerable intellect, occasionally appears somewhat emotionally backward. His fantasies and daydreams are more characteristic of a boy in his middle or late teens than of a twenty-year-old who has grown up in the shadow of the worst war in world history. In his imagination he identifies with heroes of pre-war American movies, like Clark Gable; he adores Judy Garland and Deanna Durbin, and he imagines himself to be the lover of the glamorous aristocratic German lady who inhabits a nearby manor house (an apparent fairy-tale-princess substitute).

The paradox of Danny lies in his idealistic concept of the hedonistic life-style, a paradox reminiscent of the emotional schizophrenia of the 1960s generation. Thus, his moments of religious experience, which occur at several points in the novel, are almost always mingled with intense sensuality. His prayers, generally comically naive, are seldom affected by metaphysical anxieties; they are wish-prayers for the fulfilment of his erotic desires. Danny's most extensive religious experience occurs after his brief outburst of enthusiasm for the 'revolution'; he undergoes a crisis as he becomes aware of the underlying banality of all the patriotic fervour. This sudden feeling of emotional emptiness leads him into the church in which he had frequently found comfort as a child. The church scene is characteristic not only of Danny but also of numerous other characters who appear in Škvorecký's works. Danny's religious experience is influenced greatly by his senses. He is at first discouraged by the excessive cleanness and unexpectedly bright light in the church. Eventually, he finds a dark niche decorated with a picture of the Virgin. The portrait, however, does not appear sufficiently beautiful to him: he closes his eyes and starts imagining the Virgin with the features of Irena, to whom he then whispers an ardent prayer. Gradually, the religious content of the prayer begins to wane and Irena as an erotic object takes over. Finally, his reawakened sexual desire entirely dispels his existential crisis. Yet, the final synergy is not Irena herself, but his regained trust in the future ideal love for which Irena is merely a substitute. 'Damn Irena. She's not bad, but that's only because there isn't much choice. I looked up at the altar and remembered I'd wanted to say the Lord's Prayer. I began, but what was it I'd wanted to pray about? Oh yeah, to feel something again. But I was already feeling again. I didn't need to pray anymore. I had lots of feelings now.' (p. 86)

The church episode dramatises Danny's circular emotional logic. A crisis of his hedonistic beliefs inspires in him a quest for the transcendental. However, the transcendental does not become a superior experience by itself, but represents a bridge leading towards the restoration of his sensual appreciation of life, which in turn is only another bridge towards the quasi-transcendental in the form of a fantasy. Danny is a romantic, albeit neither self-assured, nor disillusioned. He stands on the borderline between both varieties.

The contradictory and elusive aspect of Danny's character was perhaps designed by the author as a reaction to the one-dimensional heroes of the 'official' literature of the post-war period. Yet it is difficult not to feel on occasion that the contradictions of the character are allowed to go too far, at the expense of the artistic logic of the work. For example, in some parts of the novel, Danny is shown as an educated young man, well versed in foreign languages and familiar with important intellectual concepts. Indeed, he sometimes worries about being overeducated to the point of losing intellectual curiosity altogether. He regards this problem as a sign of the decadence of his class and contrasts his overeducation with the working class's voracious appetite for knowledge:

> I knew there was a hunger in those people riding past on those wagons and in those who'd be setting up the Party and discussion groups and Marxist study groups and all that – a hunger for knowledge. I'd already got to know them at the factory, from discussions we'd had in the john, and when I talked about the solar system and about galaxies and Apollinaire and American history they'd listened, wide-eyed. There was hunger in them for things I was glutted with. It was different with me. With my past and with my ancestors and education taken for granted for generations and just comfort and luxury in general. (p. 392)

On another occasion we are given a very different characterisation of Danny's education:

> I wondered if that was enough to live for, but nothing else came to my mind so I left it at that and quickly started thinking about Irena again, about one walk we'd taken through the woods one night and how awfully inferior I'd felt when she started talking about Victor Hugo and Byron and I got Byron mixed with Balzac and Balzac with Barbusse and I hadn't read anything by any of them, and it seemed to me I was as dumb as ever. (p. 132)

The Cowards 17

This contradiction can hardly be explained as Danny's changing mood. This passage also modifies the image of Irena, who is generally shown as an unreflective type, and inferior to Danny in intelligence. Much has been written about the novel's style. Henry Kučera in particular has shown that Škvorecký was an important innovator in the use of various registers of the Czech language.[5] In Czech, the difference between the literary and the colloquial languages is more pronounced than in most other European languages. This phenomenon has been defined by some linguists as a *de facto* diglossia. Pre-war Czech writers have generally dealt with the problem in a somewhat restrained manner. Karel Čapek, for example, used in his fiction colloquialisms only in lexis and syntax. He shunned the use of colloquial elements of phonology and morphology. In contrast to that approach, Škvorecký uses a huge variety of registers for stylistic purposes, and goes far beyond such pioneers in the use of Colloquial and Common Czech as Jaroslav Hašek. Moreover, his characters do not have a fixed mode of speaking, and their blend of Colloquial or Common Czech and Literary Czech alters according to their environment. Danny uses almost no Common Czech when communicating with his parents, in contrast to when he is talking to his friends, and uses very little Colloquial Czech when talking to strangers. Curiously, colloquialisms are almost absent in his interior monologues. The varied use of language significantly enhances the perception of the social atmosphere of the novel's individual episodes, but this effect virtually disappears in translation. English is governed by different principles, and to find accurate equivalents for the large number of stylistic nuances of the novel may be all but impossible.

Although published a decade after its origin, *The Cowards* was one of the major events in the post-war history of Czech literature. Not only its iconoclastic treatment of a familiar theme, but also its style, tone and structure, influenced an entire generation of Czech fiction writers. It liberated the Czech novel from an excessive dependence on plot and showed the way towards a looser, more improvisational mode. To many readers, as well as some critics, *The Cowards* is Škvorecký's masterpiece, unsurpassed by any of his later fiction. The novel has indeed a freshness and spontaneity which Škvorecký's later novels never achieved to the same degree. However, it is not difficult to see that *The Cowards* is a work of limited ambition. As the author himself has stated, originally it was not written for readers but merely for the very pleasure of writing.[6] Škvorecký's later works reach well beyond the dramatic, psychological and philosophical boundaries of his first work and, in spite of occasional misjudgements, they do so with considerable success.

2 The End of the Nylon Era

The End of the Nylon Era (*Konec nylonového věku*, 1967) is the least well known of Škvorecký's novels, one that was published in only a single edition and has never been translated into a foreign language. The timing of its origin was crucial for its fate. Written in 1950, two years after the Communist takeover, it was not harmful from the thematic viewpoint. But it was not written in the Socialist Realist mode and was therefore unpublishable until 1967, when the aesthetic dogmata of Socialist Realism were no longer enforced. This short novel (120 pages) reflects Škvorecký's ambivalent attitude towards the life-style of the affluent, an attitude which is to a lesser degree present in *The Cowards*. Although the novel is to some extent a satire, it is also a psychological profile of the Czech bourgeoisie on the eve of its demise. The satirical scope is focused narrowly, showing the pro-Western, and especially pro-American, craze by which the affluent post-war Czech youth were obsessed. They all learned English, most of them mastering only the basics, idolised jazz, and dressed in a style copied from imported fashion magazines. Škvorecký himself actively participated in this life-style, and his negative portrayal of it might indicate the effect that the official anti-American propaganda had made on him, or it may simply result from self-doubt or an ability to see himself and his environment from a critical point of view. At the same time, the portrayal is not without touches of affection for the dying way of life.

Some aspects of the novel are analogous to aspects of *The Cowards*. Time and place are once again closely delineated, and there is an absence of conventional plot. The entire novel consists in the description of a few characters who attend a ball in a prestigious Prague ballroom. However, the differences are greater than the similarities. Unlike the centralised first-person method used in *The Cowards*, *The End* is based upon a complex structure of interior monologues and *erlebte Rede*. Dialogues and expository prose are used less. The influence of Dos Passos on this novel has been acknowledged by Škvorecký himself.

The most important characters are Jiřina Kočandrlová, the daughter of a wealthy landowner; Irena Hallmanová and her husband, Robert; Samuel Gellen, Irena's admirer and suspected lover; Martin Bartoš, who has just completed his university degree in literature;

Pedro Gerswinder, a mild alcoholic; and František Stodola, an amateur saxophone player with weak lungs, who is obliquely patterned on the author himself. In keeping with their Anglo-American cultural snobbery, they seldom call each other by their Czech names, and instead use their English-language equivalents. Thus Jiřina is transformed into Georgiana, Irena into Irene, Robert into Bob, Samuel into Sam and so on.

Most of the interior monologues are preoccupied with erotic concerns. They include teenage-like yearnings, frustrated sexual drives, sado-masochistic fantasies, and jealous ravings. Jiřina is the ugly duckling of the group, and her thoughts and fantasies are coloured by her feelings of inferiority and envy towards her more attractive female friends. In her interaction with others she is preoccupied with instigating discords. Irene, her husband, Robert, and Sam are trapped in a curious triangle. Irene is a beautiful woman who had decided early in her adolescence that she would never belong to more than one man. She was a talented dancer and dreamt about a husband from America, but a heart disease had dashed her professional career, and her dreams of an exotic marriage had not come true. Irene loves her husband, while carrying on with Sam, although without allowing the sexual consummation of their affair. Because of her withdrawn nature, neither her husband nor anyone else has any knowledge of Irene's self-imposed restraint, and there are frequent scenes of jealousy within the trio. The novel ends with a brawl between Robert and Sam.

Irene is one of the most enigmatic of Škvorecký's creations, although she is portrayed only sketchily. While some aspects of her personality are reminiscent of the character with the same name in *The Cowards*, she is substantially more complex and intelligent, and has her own philosophy of life, derived from existentialism. To call her a tease would not be quite just, but she certainly exhibits narcissistic tendencies. She is sexually somewhat devious (her lesbian inclinations are hinted at in one of her monologues), but her love for Sam appears to be genuine. Her feelings of loyalty and pity for her husband Robert are also real, although not based on moral grounds.

Robert is anomalous within the group. He is the only one that has separated himself from his class and become a Communist activist. However, while having been capable of severing ideological ties to his class, he is incapable of breaking with it psychologically. He despises his former friends, has a love-hate relationship with his wife, and feels a deep contempt for his own inability to make a clean cut with his past. His dilemma contains tragic as well as comic aspects. Sam's self-doubt is different but no less intense. He is frustrated by Irene's affectionate aloofness and would like to put an end to the protracted affair, but does not have the strength to do so. He is keenly conscious of other women, but only as a reminder of his humiliating, absurd bondage.

In the disorganised, perversely twisted emotional life of the trio, the author probably wanted to epitomise the crisis of the entire bourgeoisie. Sam sees his generation as the bourgeoisie's last, finishing the gradual degenerative process of the once vital social group: 'And finally, the third generation came limping in, the decomposed and debased one, wasting its young lives in senseless adventure with the wives of other men, a generation without any mission, or ambition, and without any healthy political idiosyncrasies, and as a matter of fact, without any idiosyncrasies at all.'[1] The triumph of Communism then appears to be a logical consequence of the class's fatigue, and to be historically justified: 'The fault lies not in Bolshevism, but in us. We are permeated by senselessness, but there is nothing I can do about it. I know that Communism is a marvellous thing, marvellous for ninety-nine per cent of people, but we belong to the remaining one per cent. It is not for us'. (p. 35)

The other characters are equally unfulfilled. Martin's finishing his studies condemns him to a career as a high-school teacher in a provincial town, a prospect which he faces with profound abhorrence.

The ideologically coloured interior monologues, important as they are for conveying the principal theme, do not belong to the best passages of the novel. Many of them paraphrase well-known points of Marxist ideology; others are too functionally contrived. The most compelling parts of the work contain interior monologues which deal with mundane situations and problems of sensuality. In particular, Škvorecký shows himself to be a perspicacious observer of female sensibility. For example, the reflections of the homely, obese Jiřina during her dance with Irene's husband are traced as follows:

> Robert's moist hand was touching her back, just where her bra-button was. Why doesn't he put it somewhere else, that idiot! Oh dear, she will never ever be able to have a man! Whenever a man holds her during a dance, she feels as if she were him, as if she had his hands and were touching her own body with them. He must feel it, the abundance of fat which flows over the latex strap which

holds everything together. She cried out in her mind: No, I'll never have a man, and I don't want one either. I wouldn't believe him. I'd have to laugh at him. I'd be baffled by him. (p. 61)

Škvorecký proves himself in this work to be an accomplished master of small talk and everyday scenes, rather than a creator of broadly conceived human destinies. His second novel is less important than his first, and manifests that crisis experienced by many authors who base their first work on autobiographical material. *The End of the Nylon Era* is nevertheless a mature work which would have attracted more attention if it had been published just after it was written (in 1950). In 1967 it could be welcomed only as an interesting document of Škvorecký's artistic growth. In some respects, however, the short novel anticipates later developments in Czech literature, seen for example in the prose of Vladimír Páral. Škvorecký himself took a different route, returning in the best of his later works to the broad, freewheeling narrative style of his first novel.

3 The Tank Corps

The Tank Corps (*Tankový prapor*) was originally scheduled to appear during the final days of the Prague Spring, in early 1969. However, although most of it appeared in the periodical *Plamen*, in Czechoslovakia, its book-form publication was abruptly halted, and it was not until 1971 that it was finally printed by Škvorecký's own publishing house in Toronto. The action of the novel, according to Škvorecký, was based on his two-year stint in the Czechoslovak Army, in 1951–53, and it was allegedly completed in 1954. But it appears that the genesis of the work was somewhat more complicated than indicated by Škvorecký, and that some parts of the work were probably written at a much later date. The novel repeatedly confuses the chronology of certain important historical events of the early 1950s. It is unlikely that such distortions would have occurred if the novel had indeed been written in its entirety at the time stated by the author.

For example, there is a description of a farewell party organised by the members of the tank corps. The hall in which the festivities take place is decorated with a monstrous Byzantine collage composed of images from official iconography:

> Dusty garlands woven from paper flowers were rising at irregular intervals towards a huge red star on the front wall. On each side, the star was flanked by a picture – on the right there was President Zápotocký, and on the left General Čepička – both in uniform, and adorned with an amazing number of medals, with both of the pictures fading out in an ellipsoid pattern towards the frame into a nondescript, Milky-Way-like flat space such as was once used in daguerrotypes. Sergeant Remunda glued into the middle of the star a portrait of Stalin, and in order to fit it into the star, trimmed it a bit, top and bottom. The deceased president was hanging under the star on a cord for the sake of symmetry and for the sake of the preservation of hierarchical order.[1] (p. 222)

From the description one would conclude that the festivities were held during the lifetime of Stalin, but after the demise of Gottwald, the first Communist president of Czechoslovakia, who was succeeded by Zápotocký. This impression is reinforced by the opening oration in which the speaker delivers the obligatory invocation 'Long live

Stalin!' However, Gottwald died later than Stalin, ostensibly after having contracted pneumonia at Stalin's funeral. On the other hand, the description of the festivities is distorted by absurdities of the most hilarious kind, which might lead one to speculate whether the confusion of chronology was not deliberately planned by the author. This proposition is unlikely, however, since, as a rule, Škvorecký observes the parameters of the probable even in the most hyperbolised situations. Although not belonging to the most important prose of the author, the novel is easily the most outstanding Czech satires on military life since Hašek's *The Good Soldier Švejk*. The significance of the satire is enhanced by the fact that, as in all Communist totalitarian regimes, the military represented a microcosm of society in general. During the final years of Stalinism, this was perhaps more true than at any other period in the history of Communism. This makes one read the work also as an unusual dystopia.

Although the inclusion of the novel in the 'autobiographical' cycle has some justification, it should not be overlooked that it exhibits some significant structural differences in comparison with the earlier *The Cowards*, and the later *Miracle*, and *The Engineer of Human Souls*. *The Tank Corps* is narrated from the third-person author-observer point of view, while the other works use the *Ich-form*. More significantly, the prominence of Danny as a character is substantially reduced. He is one of the more important characters in the novel, but the narrative is not threaded around his *persona* as in *The Cowards*, nor does Danny comment on events in a manner that would be comparable to the way Škvorecký uses him in his other 'autobiographical' works. There are numerous scenes in which Danny does not take part at all, and there are no flashbacks to or reminiscences of Kostelec, an indispensable feature of most of the other novels. The main reason for Škvorecký's use of Danny in *The Tank Corps* was probably to create continuity with *The Cowards*. Only in his later works does the character of Danny regain a more general structural prominence. Still, there are some familiar constants from Škvorecký's 'autobiographical' works. For example, there is Vrchcolák, the customary parodied *alter ego* of the 'official' poet of the 1950s (who turned dissident in the 1970s), Pavel Kohout (in later works called Vrchcoláb).

The main theme of the novel is the dismal failure of the Communist system to 'break' the traditional attitudes, habits and values of the populace in the endeavour to create the New Man. This failure has been described many times before and since this novel, but the originality of Škvorecký's work lies in his limiting the description of the ideological débâcle to the area in which it manifested itself most conspicuously and perhaps also most comically, namely, in military service. Ever since the takeover in 1948, the Communist ideologues placed their greatest hope in youth. They believed that, while the 're-education' of the typical citizen might bring only limited results, young people, being unburdened by old-fashioned 'bourgeois' prejudices, would be a relatively easy target for the instilling of 'socialist morality'. Because military service put young men under the physical and psychological control of the authorities for a period of two years, considerable energy was devoted to making the time of service important not only from a military point of view, but, perhaps even more, from an ideological. The private life of the conscript was virtually eliminated. When not engaged in military training, he was exposed to massive ideological indoctrination. Military service was conceived of as a broadening, enriching experience, which would forever eradicate the residue of bourgeois ways of thinking and elevate young people to a spiritual level previously unimaginable.

The novel describes the typical young man's reaction to this grandiose design. Its premises are discredited almost from minute to minute, as it becomes obvious that they collide with the basic principles of human nature. The soldiers consider military service boring and senseless, and ideological models are either incomprehensible or ridiculous for them. They see the system as an absurdity which cannot be openly defied. The average soldier's defences are passive and paradoxical in nature. To preserve his humanity, he has to suppress his dignity by becoming as inconspicuous as possible. He puts on the mask of a clown or an idiot, because, should he appear intelligent, he would become an object of increased attention on the part of his 'perfectionist' superiors. The ultimate, inevitable collision with the utopian, Pygmalionesque ideal would become only that much more painful. The socialist army is made up of hundreds of thousands of Good Soldiers Švejk. Many, perhaps most of them, are unaware of the role they began to play once they put on their uniforms. Their reactions to the assaults on their personalities are instinctive and naive, and perhaps for this reason that much more effective.

Defiance of the system is, to a large extent, made easy by the fact that the career officers, although most of them are recruited from the politically 'dependable' segment of society, themselves lack the necessary confidence in the success of their efforts. Many of them also feel trapped by the mechanism of military life and on occasion resort to antics similar to those of the conscripts in order to escape the wrath of the staff-officers. Behind the ideological façade, the socialist army is held together by conventional ties – a hierarchy of power and fear. The comic aspect of the situation is that the higher the rank of an officer, the more distinct are his symptoms of alienation from the socialist ideal. Frustrated by the futility of their efforts, many of the high-ranking officers resort to senseless intimidation. Others, the more honest of them, suffer from feelings of inferiority and guilt, as they do not quite realise that their failure is caused not by their personal shortcomings, but by the inherent fallacy of the theoretical assumptions they are required to follow.

The official renunciation of the mechanical division of the army into privates, non-commissioned officers and officers, and the substitution of this principle by mutual respect and collaboration, proves unworkable not just because in military life authority without fear is ineffective, but also because the new principle deprives those in command of the gratification derived from the administration of power. However, no matter whether power is applied out of enjoyment or out of necessity, it is clad in the garb of Communist ideology. Even though some officers are aware that the lack of enthusiasm on the part of the soldiers has little to do with those officers' ability to win them over by the art of political persuasion, they use ideological arguments as a device for forcing obedience. The fact that the report on the performance of each individual in his military service becomes a permanent part of his confidential file, significantly influencing his post-military career, is a compelling factor in the behaviour of most soldiers. The higher the level of education a given conscript has, the greater his ambition for the future, and, thus also, the greater his difficulty in coping with the system.

The novel does not develop any coherent story or plot. It consists simply of independent situations, suggested by the titles of the nine individual chapters, such as 'The Seventh Tank Corps Attacking the Defences of the Enemy', 'A Night in the Stockade', or 'The Scent of Civilian Life'. The chapters are frequently broken up into scenes, some of which resemble simple straightforward skits. Two chapters, from a milieu outside the barracks, describe Danny's unsuccessful attempts to have an affair with a seductive, but reluctant young woman.

Most of the depictions of military life consist of episodes highlighting the breakdown of discipline in the chain of command. Relatively most efficient is the administration of discipline in the senior ranks, where there is normally one-to-one contact. But as an order reaches the lower ranks, it gradually loses its weight. There is more than one reason for this phenomenon, as the novel shows. Among the higher ranks, an order is merely an abstract concept. When it is to be acted upon, it becomes more and more concrete, and therefore less and less practicable or even comprehensible. Also, the closer an order comes to the level of the simple soldier, the more it is diluted by the sheer number of individuals who are supposed to follow it. A chain of command resembles the flow of a powerful river, which branches into a delta and is finally absorbed by sand. In the first chapter of the novel, portraying early-morning manoeuvres, for example, the military juggernaut is reduced to a spluttering Heath-Robinson contraption as a direct result of the gradual dilution of discipline.

Škvorecký shows in a masterly fashion how military life consists in words and ritual rather than action. Army life is often not much more than a verbose show performed by third-rate actors who have no confidence in their own abilities. In spite of their intensely farcical character, some scenes in *The Tank Corps* have an almost eerie quality. For example, the night exercises described in the first chapter resemble a grotesque rehearsal of amateurs in *A Midsummer Night's Dream*. Some episodes of the novel would probably bewilder not only a foreign reader, but even a native Czech unfamiliar with the life-style of the 1950s. In particular chapter 2, describing the examinations for the Julius Fučík Prize may, perhaps, be fully appreciated only by those who have personal experience of the Stalin era. The objective of the competition was to introduce young readers to the cream of Socialist Realist fiction. Successful performance in the examination not only secured a prize, but was also a valuable demonstration of political readiness for post-military careers. The novel treats the examination as another example of the hopeless conflict between an abstract design and human nature. To the average conscript, the ideological tenets of the works discussed are remote, and he reacts to the text in an unexpectedly subjective way, if at all. Thus a discussion of the socialist concept of female virtue is quickly concretised by the soldiers into an eloquent, heated debate on the properties of the female body. An attempt to have one conscript summarise in simple language the plot of a novel they have all just finished reading results in a stream of disjointed words and sounds, which reminds us of the Absurdist works of Ionesco or Beckett.

The basic conflicts of the novel are repeated in various forms. Official, waxworks dignity and solemnity clash with the unruly and irreverent nature of the young men. Marxist doctrine competes poorly with their erotic fantasies and sentimental daydreams. The collision between the two worlds is frequently developed not just psychologically, but in satirically exaggerated caricatures. Thus one scene portrays a session devoted to literature which consists of recitations of Socialist Realist panegyric. The poem extolling the fervour of Communist soldiers fuses with a profane song being sung by a group outside the barracks who have no knowledge of what is going on inside. The situation gradually grows into a symbolic contest between official, empty pomposity and instinctive, crude vitality; the latter emerges triumphant. The bombastic rhetoric is almost completely drowned by the dirty song.

Škvorecký was taken to task by some émigré critics for the crudeness of the novel's language. In comparison with *The Cowards*, the language contains considerably more slang, vulgarisms, and downright obscenities. Yet one hardly ever feels that the scatological style transgresses the boundaries of the novel's overall artistic design. The question is not whether the novel's portrayal of the soldiers' language is true to life – there can be no doubt that it is – but rather whether the deviation from literary language performs an aesthetically meaningful function. Škvorecký could hardly have used a better device for making the conflict between reality and the artificial design of the military establishment more palpable than through language. The clash is reflected in the wooden verbosity of the officers which is contrasted with the profanities of the conscripts, for whom sexual and scatological language constitutes an emotional release, and makes for yet another weapon for the preservation of their individuality. Some of the expressions from the anal and erotic spheres are in fact extraordinarily imaginative (all, according to Škvorecký, pasted together from real life), and the points in the dialogues containing vulgarisms and obscenities are adroitly phrased and timed. At their best, they remind one of the linguistic virtuosity of David Mamet. In spite of Škvorecký's success in employing scatological jargon, from his later works it becomes evident that he is most at ease when using a circumlocutious, suggestive, Boccacio-like style when dealing with 'delicate subjects'.

The characters are simplified to the point of caricature, or else are developed only episodically, without any attempt at psychological depth. Such a treatment is understandable in a work that aims to present a broad, impressionistic tableau which has primarily satirical objectives. The dominant character of the novel is Major Borovička, the highest ranking officer the novel presents in any detail. Borovička, nicknamed Little Devil (*Malinký ďábel*) because of his diminutive stature but ferocious militarism, epitomises military power at its worst. Borovička, who had been a sergeant-major prior to the Communist takeover, was, thanks to his political affiliation, catapulted to the undreamt-of position of staff officer. He is motivated less by ideological conviction than by the sheer enjoyment of exercising his power to humiliate those under his command. He takes sadistic pleasure in enforcing minor rules, and is perennially preoccupied by looking for mistakes on the part of both conscripts and officers. He is a master of Communist ideological jargon, which he applies in all possible situations. Building on the method he first tested in *The Cowards*, Škvorecký uses the device of contrasting the physical properties of a character, here Borovička, with the position of power he occupies. Borovička has a high-pitched, squeaky voice, bizarre short legs and arms, and his stature is likened to that of a midget. He moves around like a spectre, appearing unexpectedly in the most unlikely places.

Škvorecký makes profuse use of diminutives when referring to this character, a device which is totally lost in translation. Diminutives, which are mostly used hypocoristically, are in Czech typically formed by suffixes: *ruce–ručičky*, *boty–botičky* (the translation 'hands'– 'dear little hands', 'shoes'– 'dear little shoes' does not do justice to the nuances). However, in the context of the novel, they are used for the opposite purpose, to create in the reader a feeling of almost physical disgust, which is augmented by the frenetic, robot-like mobility of the minute parts of which Borovička is composed.

Other officers are treated more benevolently by the author. Captain Matka, a former insurance clerk, was induced to enter military service by expectations of a more glamorous life. He learned to regret his decision profoundly, as he finds no gratification in the everyday routine of the army. He derives little satisfaction from bullying others, and recalls with nostalgia his civilian life in which he had occupied, due to his political affiliation, a distinguished post. Also without rancour is the portrayal of the political officer (*politruk*), Lieutenant Prouza, an idealist who has failed to recognise the futility of his task of moulding the troops into an ideologically mature body.

Danny stands out as a character among the conscripts. Far from being typical, he was drafted into the army after he had received a doctorate in philosophy and is therefore more a target of his superiors' attention than the typical conscript. His knowledge of the dependence of his future career upon a favourable report on his military service has made him 'a timid fellow, and therefore obedient'. Danny is one of the least Švejkesque of the soldiers, and comparisons of him to Hašek's hero are misleading. He seems to be well-liked, but he is clearly not quite the same as the others. Perhaps the crucial episode as far as Danny's relative unusualness is concerned is the Chaplinesque scene describing Danny's predilection for polishing his boots, an activity which is detested by other soldiers. For Danny, polishing his boots becomes a moment of independence, a means for the assertion of his individuality and aesthetic consciousness in a world of intolerable vulgarity. Other conscripts remain in the reader's memory as heroes (or rather anti-heroes) of specific scenes, rather than as consistently developed individuals.

The novel has some weaknesses. Despite the fact that the events described took place during the worst period of the Stalin era, the overall impression one derives from the narrative is that, regardless of all the adverse features, if looked at with detachment, military service was fun, which, of course, it was not. This impression is caused by the author's indecision about whether to develop the work as fully-fledged satire or as satire interspersed with true-to-life scenes and comedy for its own sake. Moreover, many scenes are overlong and too detailed. It is as if the author had not been able to separate the wheat from the chaff. The two chapters that take place outside the barracks (Danny's leave) have no structural justification in the novel. On occasion, the humour becomes tasteless, particularly in certain portrayals of 'negative' characters; this changes the tone of the narrative in an obtrusive way. The ending of the novel is a case in point, where 'Little Devil' is made to suffer an ignominious death. After he has failed to stop the soldiers' unruly farewell party, Borovička falls (or is he pushed?) into the cess-pit leading from the barracks' latrine. The death is discovered long after the incident, when the sewer pump is clogged by a small riding boot that is identified as having belonged to the midget major. Borovička's drowning in the excrement of his troops constitutes artificial and crude symbolism, and as a melodramatic element in the action, it is in disharmony with the novel's overall method. Another bizarre incident, an attempted suicide by a conscript, also takes place in the latrines. The attempt fails, when the belt on which the soldier attempts to hang himself, breaks under his weight, and he falls into the lavatory bowl. Škvorecký's fascination with the lavatorial, which becomes less artificial and crude in his later works, commences with *The Tank Corps*. Although banned in Czechoslovakia during the past twenty years, the novel became one of the most popular works of Czech literature. Copied and recopied by hand, it became a cult object, especially among the Czechoslovak conscripts.

4 The Lion Cub

Like all Škvorecký's novels *The Lion Cub* (*Lvíče*) has a complicated publication history. Written and re-written during the years 1964–67, the work was originally scheduled to be published in 1966. However, it appeared only in 1969, in an edition of 40 000 copies, and it was immediately bought up by the reading public. The second printing, in almost double the quantity of the original edition, missed the end of the Dubček era by only a few days. The new régime ordered that all copies be immediately confiscated and subsequently destroyed. In 1974 Škvorecký republished the novel in his publishing house in Canada. The English translation appeared in the same year under the title *Miss Silver's Past*.

The novel is a blend of love story, murder mystery, and satire (with elements of a *roman à clef*). Gleb Žekulin regarded its description of the moral disintegration of Communist society in the pre-Dubček era as the work's principal purpose.[1] He believed that the melodramatic element was used merely as a camouflage for its essentially satirical and moralising orientation. In his introduction to the English translation, Škvorecký himself provides ample grounds for this interpretation: 'I decided to make it look like light literature, like an entertainment, although the subject was so bloody serious. To make it a melodrama, a debased genre, so that it would escape the attention of the man with the rubber stamp, and make the aesthete wonder why the author of *The Cowards* and *The Bass Saxophone* was writing a crime story about such an improbable sexbomb as Miss Silver . . . Was it because he wanted to please the crowds?'[2]

As so often, Škvorecký's commentary should be taken with a grain of salt. His interest in 'debased genres', particularly the tale of mystery, is by no means limited to his pre-exile period. During his exile, it has actually been more pronounced than before, in spite of the fact that the author has no longer had to be concerned with the intrusion of the censor. *Sins for Father Knox* (*Hříchy pro pátera Knoxe*, 1973), as well as the sequel to the Lieutenant Borůvka cycle, almost entirely written in exile, are either pure or parody detective stories. So *The Lion Cub* should be viewed rather as a transitional work in which Škvorecký begins to test more complex structures. In his exile novels, the melodramatic element becomes an important aspect of his aesthetics, one which sets very broad objectives for itself. The entertainment element is strikingly present in most of his mature works, and the author frequently emphasises this aspect. *The Engineer of Human Souls* (*Inženýr lidských duší*, 1977) is expressly (albeit semi-fascetiously) subtitled 'An Entertainment', while *Miracle* (*Mirákl*, 1972) is in part a detective novel. Škvorecký's blending of genres appears to be part of his attempt to break through the limitations of the *Ich-form*. While this narrative method is the most suitable for his talent, allowing a subjective selection of facts articulated with a distinct 'voice', it tends to restrict the narrative scope and to result in monotony. The deliberate, frequently playful blending of genres is Škvorecký's way of adding another dimension to the narrative canon. In comparison with *The Engineer* and *Miracle*, *The Lion Cub* is a structurally disciplined work. That does not necessarily mean that it is superior to his exile novels. This novel is much more self-conscious in its weaving together of narrative strands, and a far cry from the uninhibited narrative verve of *Miracle* and *The Engineer*.

The three levels of the novel – the love story, the murder mystery, and the satire – are not developed with equal scope and intensity. The largest part of the work is composed of the love story; the satirical scenes take second place. The detective story occupies only a small segment of the narrative – in fact, the reader is not aware that he is reading a detective story until the very end, when the focus unexpectedly changes.

The novel is a first-person narrative related by the young editor of a literary journal, Karel Leden. The fact that Škvorecký uses a narrative *persona* other than Danny Smiřický is not without significance. Smiřický is an openly autobiographical character, who is usually accompanied by other characters modelled on friends from the author's youth, some of whom appear for the first time in *The Cowards*. Excursions into Smiřický's youth in the form of flashbacks are common. However, no such method is employed in *The Lion Cub*. The autobiographical element is noticeable, but it is derived entirely from Škvorecký's adult life, when he, like Leden, was an editor in a publishing house. As a character, Leden is, to some degree, similar to Smiřický. Both have non-tragic, anti-heroic stances towards life, but while Smiřický is generally portrayed as a commonsense pragmatist and sceptic, Leden is more of a cynic. The very surname Leden (January), though not too uncommon in Czech, was undoubtedly chosen to suggest the cool, detached, calculating nature of the narrator. But then Smiřický is no paragon of spontaneity either, and, in particular, the two characters' attitudes to women are similar.

The love story concerns Leden's infatuation with a beautiful young zoologist, Lenka Stříbrná (Silver). In summary the story goes as follows: Leden has a friend, Vašek Žamberk, a teacher of physical education, who is intellectually somewhat limited. Žamberk has a debilitating inferiority complex towards women, and is allegedly a virgin, despite his being thirty years old. Leden, who is a notorious seducer, has in the past repeatedly acted as a point man for Žamberk, but all such attempts have ended in a fiasco. The action begins on a river bank, where Leden is once again to act as a companion at a rendezvous with Žamberk's latest object of admiration, Lenka Stříbrná. The young woman surprises Leden by being not only strikingly beautiful, but also intellectually far superior to his friend. He instantly decides to reverse the roles, to use Žamberk as a tool for conquering Lenka himself. A lucky accident appears to play into his hands. Žamberk, who has nothing to offer besides his physical prowess, makes himself look ridiculous when he almost drowns in the river after an attack of cramp. To his eternal embarrassment, he is saved thanks to Lenka who, with the help of Leden, manages to pull him out of the water.

Leden, who is used to easy conquests, expects to seduce Lenka on the first day, but he runs into determined resistance. The young woman is immediately aware of his superficial interest in women, and refuses to be just another sex object. During subsequent meetings, she tolerates him as a companion, but keeps him at arm's length. Leden, well versed in amorous tactics, tries various masks and poses (some of them textbook applications of *ars amandi*), but fails miserably. Finally, he becomes the victim of his own intrigues, and falls in love with the resistant woman. However, either because of her distrust of him, or for other, unexplained reasons, Lenka continues to treat him with cool, though occasionally flirtatious, indifference. Leden's frustration is so great that once he even tries to overwhelm her by brute force, only to be painfully injured by her, thanks to her knowledge of male anatomy. And Leden's humiliation does not end there: while he is away for two months on military duty as a reservist, Lenka becomes Žamberk's mistress, and on his return, she is about to marry him.

This story of unrequited love contains elements of morality as well as comedy. Leden frequently resembles an archetypal melodramatic villain. His cynical scheming aimed at humiliating Žamberk while feigning friendship, and his calculated manoeuvres to conquer Lenka, sometimes resemble scenes from a conventional seduction melodrama. Leden's cynical monologues reinforce this analogy. His repeated statements concerning Lenka's planned seduction are particularly reminiscent of this genre ('this time I'm gonna get you', 'now I've trapped you, little flower', and so on). The narrative abounds in Leden's proud assertions of a cynicism that is raised to the level of a world-view. For example, he comments on his decision to steal Lenka from Žamberk:

> Healthy egoism prevailed . . . Yes, Vašek is a pal, but how many friendships have been betrayed because of women. And so when I realised that there are extensive precedents for my duplicity, my conscience became immediately clear. Anyhow, I am sacrificing an ethical principle for an urgent desire, which is the most excusable sacrifice in the world.[3] (p. 32)

On the other hand, the tone of the utterances, and the circumstances surrounding them, make Leden look more like a parody of the melodrama villain. No doubt the author wished to portray him as a corrupt individual, but there are elements in his portrayal that lean more to the tradition of the likeable rogue. The comic, occasionally grotesque, pattern of the story contributes to this impression. The subplot of the love story is written almost entirely in the comic vein. Leden has a girl-friend, Věra, who is cast in the role of an ingénue. Her defenceless naïveté contrasts with the experience and self-confidence of Lenka. She is a foil to Lenka, as Žamberk is a foil to Leden. However, Věra's blind loyalty to Leden, who uses her only when frustrated with his attempts to seduce Lenka, finally runs its course. She avenges herself by having an affair of her own, and, to the utmost humiliation of Leden, with none other than the much-despised Žamberk. Leden thus feels doubly disgraced.

Pure situation comedy is also present in the narrative. Thus Věra becomes (twice!) an accidental witness of Leden's semi-comic, semi-serious pleadings for Lenka's mercy; on both occasions he kneels on the pavement. Outright slapstick can also be found, such as the dropping of food on womens' new dresses by their awkward companions. There are verbal duels between Leden and Lenka, in which she assumes the role of a Molièresque 'raisonneur', chastising the attitudes and manners of her male suitor. Normally Leden counters these invectives with uncannily effective sophistry.

While being light reading, the love story has enough psychological interest and narrative grace to stand on its own. But it is the satirical element which raises the novel to a serious level. The satire is woven into the narrative through the narrator's occupation. In his youth, Leden had written a collection of love poems which, while admittedly not a model product of Socialist Realism, was favourably received by establishment critics. Leden was made a member of the state-controlled Writers' Union, and, after he had finished his university studies, was given a highly respectable position as editor of a state-run publishing house. As an author, Leden lives entirely on his past reputation. After the publication of his early lyric verse, his literary activity was limited to occasional versifying to celebrate official heroes and potentates or to attack the Western way of life. Deep in his heart, however, Leden is an anti-establishment man who knows that the Communist ideal, in which he had believed when he was young, has been irreparably compromised. He justifies his present literary activity with a type of 'prudent' cynicism, similar to his attitudes to love and friendship:

> When one is young and green, one resents the fact that the world is full of injustice, hypocrisy and falsehood and one yearns for beautiful girls, adventure and all sorts of silly stuff. Later, one loses it all, cools one's desire for girls by following the advice of St. Paul and by going to movies, and the urge for adventure is replaced by reading detective stories and watching sports events because, when one makes money, one may indulge in a great deal of foolishness. Those two or three individuals who remained virgins in the figurative, nonsexual sense, turn into real poets. And a few others whom the world has deprived of all forms of virginity, turns into male or female whores. As for myself, it was clear – and I accepted it without any regrets – that I belonged to the third category, but by no means to the very top. (p. 44)

Leden is a member of the editorial board that decides which works will be published and which rejected. During the Stalinist era, the decision-making process was simple: the directives from above were unambiguous and promulgated by a handful of cultural bosses, who in turn slavishly followed Russian models. The fall of the Stalin cult threw everything into turmoil. The decision-making process became much less centralised, which left Prague's ideological dogmatists in a vacuum. What was allowed, and what forbidden, ceased to be a certainty. The novel does not describe the ideological chaos at the top of the pyramid. The editorial board is analogous to the middle management of a corporate structure. We receive only indirect information about the truly mighty and powerful. One such distant, unseen potentate is appropriately named Král (King). The very sound of his name makes some of the members of the editorial board shudder. The function of the board is not to formulate theories, but to implement them. However, the vagueness of the new directives – the cultural bosses themselves are seemingly reluctant to be precise for fear of running counter to trends in Moscow – caused the fragmentation of the once monolithic board into factions. Besides the relatively greater subjective interpretation of Marxist aesthetics, the ebbing of fear also plays a role. During Stalinism, opposition to the official line was a sure way to the labour camp or worse. Under Khrushchev, the repercussions became much less severe.

To some board members, Leden included, the new freedom is a burden. 'With nostalgia I recalled the time, when our language was yes, yes, no, no. There were no struggles for anything', he comments. (p. 56) The Stalinist era is perceived by them as a time of perverse innocence, when disputes were limited to such trivia as whether or not a publication of works by nineteenth-century Czech classic authors should include illustrations. Politically more delicate questions were also solved with ease. Thus the Czech edition of *Uncle Tom's Cabin* became an adaptation with topical overtones, rather than a translation of the original. The ideological retouching resulted in Uncle Tom's appearing like some forerunner of a left-wing trade-union leader.

In the past, the board was run with an iron fist by its chief, Procházka, one of the key characters of the novel. Before the Communist takeover, Procházka had been far from a left-wing radical. In his youth he had written religious poetry, under the influence of the Marian cult. He had married into a rich family, but after the takeover, he quickly realised that the movement of history had become unfavourable to the old ruling class, and he changed colours. He divorced his bourgeois wife, and married the daughter of a high-ranking Party official. Through this connection, he gained the coveted position of editor-in-chief, which assured him not only a high salary, but also numerous privileges, such as vacationing at special resorts.

Procházka is totally corrupt, an extreme version of Leden. Endowed with an uncanny talent for distinguishing long-term political trends from temporary ideological aberrations, he is a master tactician in the bureaucratic world. 'Our chief always reacted to historical contexts', says Leden, who serves as a sort of commentator on Procházka. (p. 7) He is an ideological Proteus to whom adjustment to circumstances is not an act of opportunism, but a moral value. He is perennially in flux, not only as far as his views are concerned, but even in his social habits. During the Stalinist years, for instance, he modelled even his appearance upon the pattern of a hard-working *chinovnik*, and wore shabby clothes. During the Khrushchev Thaw, he began to wear fashionable, elegant clothes, in conformity with the new official Party line. However, he views the euphoria in cultural politics of the late 1950s with extreme caution. He is convinced that the liberal trend will prove to be of short duration. He also understands that being too liberal is inherently more perilous than being too conservative. Should the Thaw continue, he reasons, he would be much more readily forgiven by the liberals than, in the event that the Thaw came to an end, he would be by the conservatives.

The satirical subplot consists of a detailed portrayal of the behaviour patterns of the members of the board, who are shown in various situations. The central scenes take place in the meeting room of the publishing house, but the narrative also follows the board members to private parties, and finally to a vacation resort. The plot revolves around the attempts of a new young editor, Dagmar Blumenfeldová, to push through the publication of a novel by an unknown female author, Cibulková. The manuscript, entitled *Among Us Girls*, is a true-to-life story set in the milieu of hedonistic Czech youth, and is essentially devoid of Socialist Realist elements. Had the manuscript been submitted a few years earlier, Procházka would have rejected it without any discussion whatsoever. The post-Stalinist trend, however, made such summary decisions impossible, and a formal vote by the entire board had become a necessity. Blumenfeldová, an idealist endowed with quintessential female shrewdness, becomes a genuine challenge to Procházka, who opposes the publication of the work for fear of possible repercussions. Since Blumenfeldová realises that she cannot outfox Procházka on the level of political intrigues, she decides to pursue her goal by winning over the majority to her side by means of sexual temptation. She is a reasonably attractive woman, and thus indeed manages to 'persuade' several male board members of known conservative leanings to support the publication of the controversial book. Procházka, who is aware of the situation, decides to embark on delaying tactics, hoping that the inexperienced young editor will sooner or later commit a blunder that will turn everything around. His expectations are fulfilled when Blumenfeldová, while on a short trip to Moscow, is discredited by befriending two Russian anti-dogmatists, who shortly thereafter become the target of official criticism. After this incident, Procházka has no trouble convincing the board to vote overwhelmingly for the suppression of the novel.

The Procházka-Blumenfeldová struggle has several peripateias, and its outcome, albeit not unexpected, is in doubt for a long time. The descriptions of the board meetings show Škvorecký at his best. The grotesque rhetoric, the scheming and counter-scheming, the weird physical mannerisms of the characters, all have touches of Swiftian satire. Leden's posture is that of dispassionate observer. On the one hand, he sympathises with Blumenfeldová's effort but, on the other, he feels that there is much to be said in favour of his boss's attitude. The resolution of the conflict is most welcome to him: he was not forced to decide for whom he would cast his vote. Leden is not a man who thrives on conflicts. His philosophy of life is one of non-commitment.

Although *The Lion Cub* was obviously not intended to be an allegory, one is nevertheless tempted to view the bizzare publishing house as a microcosm of intellectual society of post-Stalinist Czechoslovakia. The bureaucrat Procházka is a pillar of the régime, while the 'Hebrew warrior', Blumenfeldová, prefigures the quixotic reformists of the Prague Spring. Leden and others stand for the spineless majority that is carried back and forth by the currents of history. However, Škvorecký's judgement on individual characters is, as usual, ambivalent. Blumenfeldová no doubt has Škvorecký's sympathy, but her prostitution, though in the service of a noble cause, is prostitution nonetheless. Leden, in spite of his passive opportunism, is never expressly condemned by the author. Even the corrupt Procházka has some redeeming features, despite his being portrayed overwhelmingly as a repulsive character. This avowed anti-Semite, an alcoholic womaniser with a 'lascivious smile', allegedly did not participate in the gravest excesses of the régime during the Stalinist years. He genuinely believes in the positive aspect of his anti-liberal activity and regards himself as the saviour of many individuals from serious consequences, which he is convinced will inevitably follow after the Thaw has run its course. Škvorecký's aesthetics developed too much in opposition to the yes-or-no principles of Socialist Realism. There are seldom unequivocal moral judgements in his work.

The novel turns into a detective story on page 239 of the 269-page book (in the Czech exile version). The parodistic or semi-parodistic use of the genre is immediately evident when the author signals the forthcoming crisis in boldface letters, in an advertisement-like announcement in the manner of Ellery Queen, warning the reader: 'Soon a tragedy will strike. You have been supplied with clues already. But beware – in a detective story, guessing is not enough. You have to deduce from facts'. Hardly any reader, however, would have suspected from the text itself that the novel is a detective story, let alone have watched for clues. In retrospect, the reader might recognise some motifs as possible clues, but their significance in the narrative context continues to appear of no consequence. The usual sequence of a tale of mystery is inverted. The work does not start with a crime, after which the narrative gradually develops the theme of search towards the unravelling of the mystery. The mystery becomes more or less a postscript to the narrative which provides the love story with a second ending.

The setting for the mystery is a resort, frequented by members of the Writers' Union and their families and friends. Most of the main characters are spending their weekend at the resort. They include Leden, Lenka, Žamberk, Blumenfeldová, Procházka, Cibulková, some members of the editorial board, as well as a few official cultural luminaries. During a drunken party, several scandalous scenes take place that create suspense, the most prominent being a brawl between Procházka and Cibulková. After that turbulent scene, the rejected young female author spends the night with the obligingly comforting Leden. In the morning, the visitors are stunned by shocking news: on the shore of the nearby lake a dead body has been found, apparently washed up by the waves. The body is identified as Procházka's. The police at first suspect foul play, but when Leden provides a foolproof alibi for Cibulková, the death is judged an accident. Since the former editor-in-chief had been seen getting into a rowboat late at night while drunk, it is assumed that he had fallen overboard and drowned.

Leden at first sees no reason to doubt the official theory. However, he soon begins to realise that there are inconsistencies in the accounts of witnesses. Using Holmesian analytical logic, he arrives at the conclusion that Procházka's death had not been an accident, but murder. He follows several clues that lead him to the identity of the murderer, who is none other than Lenka Stříbrná. The most important clue to this discovery is her past, which he unravels piece by piece. As Leden finds out, originally her name was Silberstein, and she had spent her childhood years in a German concentration camp. Before the war, her sister, fifteen years older, had been engaged to Procházka, who had abandoned her when the Germans had occupied Czechoslovakia. As a result of his betrayal, Lenka's sister was taken to a concentration camp, where she perished. Lenka grew up with the idea that after the war she would avenge her sister, blaming her unscrupulous fiancé for her death. However, when the war was over she did not follow up this idea, and actually tried to do her best to conceal her own Jewishness. She changed her name, removed her tattoo from her forearm, and made it a habit not to discuss her past. She met Procházka accidentally, and only gradually realised that this was the man who had indirectly caused her sister's death. Her past plan was thus revived, and she probably even became Procházka's mistress in order to set him up for the execution.

Just a few days before the scheduled wedding of Lenka to Žamberk, Leden confronts her with his discovery, and uses it as a device to extort sexual favours from her. The novel ends with Lenka's offering herself with surprisingly little resistance. The final scene of the novel is deliberately muted, so that it is not entirely clear whether Leden takes advantage of the opportunity, or whether he chooses to refrain from the consummation of the affair, in order to achieve a moral victory over the young woman, who had humiliated him repeatedly in the past by her posture of moral supremacy. Judging from Leden's past conduct, the first alternative is the more likely. But Leden's narrative, filled with Dostoyevskyan emotional ambivalence, leaves enough room for either interpretation: 'I avenged myself on you, my lily of the valley; forgive me; it was rotten of me, but I love you madly. I had to have my revenge. Forgive me ... It was Thursday, it was night, and it was the end of my love-affair with the beautiful Miss Silver ...' (p. 269)

The shift to the detective genre is effortless, thanks to the consistency in the easy-going narrative tone. Nevertheless, the ending does not adequately resolve the structural problems of the novel. Apart from the satire, which has its own independent significance and development, attention is focused on Leden and, perhaps even more, on Lenka. The curiosity of the reader as regards the narrator is reasonably satisfied thanks to the extensive introspective passages and the consistency of Leden's behaviour. Actually, half-way through the novel Leden becomes a somewhat predictable character. Lenka, though, is much more intriguing, and one's interest in her personality is never fully satisfied. The reader's disappointment is magnified by the narrator's deliberate emphasis on the enigmatic aspect of the woman. Lenka's mysterious nature is built up both by the plot and by descriptive comments. Her eyes are usually hidden behind reflecting sunglasses, and when she takes them off, the narrator is startled by their appearance: 'black eyes, without any irises – perhaps impossible, according to the laws of human anatomy'. (p. 17) They are compared to bakelite, to black buttons, 'inscrutable black buttons'. (p. 243) Throughout the novel, there is a proliferation of uncommon observations, usually linked with an elaborate use of metaphors: 'It occurred to me that if she stood here naked, she would look like a brown marble statue. An elastic, warm, kinetic statue' (p. 21); 'I had the feeling that behind the brown silk of her temple there pulsated a tiny vein' (p. 35); 'Miss Silver was a pink-and-white striped enigma' (p. 36); 'An embodiment of mystery' (p. 37); 'A unique phenomenon' (p. 36), and so on.

The devices are melodramatic, but the interest in the psychology of the character goes beyond that of a conventional tale of mystery, despite Škvorecký's disclaimer in this regard. Because of the greater-than-usual psychological depth of the novel, however, the motive for the murder becomes improbable and even absurd. Furthermore, the unresolved questions regarding Lenka are not limited to the murder. For example, her choice of Žamberk as her future husband is puzzling. One wonders whether it is due to her search for security as a result of her tormented past. That may be so, but on other occasions she certainly never strikes one as an insecure person. Even more intriguing is the willingness of this proud, headstrong woman to succumb to Leden's extortion in the final part of the narrative. The first-person point of view serves to conceal the unresolved structural problems of the novel. It can be argued, as Žekulin does, that logically the narrator's point of view has to result in a limited understanding of other character's psychology. However, Leden cannot be a convincing Holmes – who, after all, solves his mysteries with the help of his psychological insight – and remain at the same time a puzzled observer of Lenka's enigmatic personality, forever barred from penetrating her 'bakelite eyes'. The various layers of the work do not form an entirely coherent whole, and the narrative tone, although casual, is not so effectively casual (it is in Škvorecký's later many-layered novels) as to make one pass over these inconsistencies with indifference.

5 Miracle

Miracle (*Mirákl*, 1972) was Škvorecký's first novel to be written in exile. The work was published by Škvorecký's own publishing house and it immediately became one of the most popular as well as one of the most controversial of his works. It touched off heated debates in the Czech émigré community and in Czechoslovakia's intellectual underground, primarily because of the author's irreverent, iconoclastic treatment of the short-lived Prague Spring. The novel was seen by some as a radical departure from Škvorecký's earlier work because of its openly political, not to say polemical orientation. Such a view, however, is only partly justified. While Škvorecký introduces lengthy, overtly ideological passages in *Miracle*, he remains essentially faithful to his earlier rejection of all closed systems and abstract concepts and continues to be an advocate of an empirical approach to life. The objective of *Miracle* is in many ways analogous to that of his first novel, *The Cowards*, whose significant aspect was its debunking of the patriotic myth of the Czech anti-German resistance movement.

The 600-page novel is a complex blend of heterogeneous elements, a blend much more elaborate than its immediate predecessor, *The Lion Cub*, and with its monumental design it initiates a new phase in Škvorecký's aesthetics. It is by turns a mystery-melodrama, a stylised autobiography, a semi-historical and semi-fictional account of the twenty-year history of Czechoslovakia under Communism, a satire on and a pamphlet against radicalism of all kinds and, last but not least, a brilliant hodgepodge of miscellaneous anecdotes. Responding to some of his critics' negative comments on the supposedly haphazard form, Škvorecký gave in his *Self-Dig Book* the following defiant response about his moulding of the novel's structure:

> I went about the work in the following fashion: I jotted down various episodes, dialogues, and wisecracks on little pieces of paper and then I proceeded in a manner akin to assembling a jigsaw puzzle – the images cut into hundreds of irregular pieces which one plays with to kill time when afflicted by a cold. I pushed around the pieces of paper on my rug, attempting to put them into an order that would make sense. On some occasions I cut the pieces of paper in half, like, for example, the one referring to the peasant newly-wed wife whose husband, consumed with passion,

cut off the very tip of her nose. I put half the episode at the beginning, and the second half at the very end, and I was curious whether such an insignificant but, as I believed, charming story, would have sufficient cohesiveness to create, after some 500 pages of historical events, immediate recall in the mind of the reader. In this manner I created a sort of a basis, which resembled a bulletin board . . . I do not know whether it is amorphous or whether it is clever. But what I wanted to achieve by this mishmash is quite simple: I wanted to suggest – like so many before me – the basic character of the sensations with which our century bombards the human psyche. The unbelievable agglomeration of collisions, of comically catastrophic sensations, with which our lives are filled.[1]

There are basically three major movements in the novel, with numerous secondary movements intertwined at irregular intervals. The work consists of twelve chapters ranging in length from thirty to eighty pages. The chapters are divided into subchapters whose average length is three or four pages. Some consecutive subchapters develop a coherent narrative, but typically the narrative flow shifts rapidly from one movement to another. To complicate the matter still further, the events of which each movement is comprised are not presented in a chronological order. Sometimes they are presented in an inverted sequence, and sometimes impressionistically, without any temporal order at all.

Miracle is a first-person narrative related by the author's fictitious alias, Danny Smiřický. Two historical focal points separated by some twenty years form the poles between which the narrative moves back and forth. Half the action takes place during the year 1968 and immediately thereafter, but almost equal space is devoted to events that took place in 1949, when Smiřický was still in his mid twenties. These two years were significant milestones in Czech history. The year 1949 was the first year after the Communist takeover, the year during which the totalitarian régime consolidated its power by mass arrests, trials and other forms of harassment. The period of Stalinism was followed by the prolonged period of varyingly vernal Thaw that culminated in 1968 with the ill-fated attempt to transform Communism into a form of government that would follow humanitarian principles. While the principal character's (Smiřický's) narrative is limited almost exclusively to these two short time spans, scattered throughout the novel there are narratives-within-narratives from other characters about events that took place during the intervening twenty years.

The author goes a long way towards establishing a continuity of character between this version of Smiřický and his predecessors in the author's earlier works. Smiřický is now a forty-three-year-old bachelor, an author of popular fiction and musicals, who has extensive connections with prominent circles in Prague society, including other writers, politicians and members of the secret police. The intellectually undistinguished yet socially important position of Smiřický was chosen by Škvorecký with great care. On the one hand, it makes Smiřický credible as a source of information about historical events, while, on the other hand, it facilitates Škvorecký's favourite narrative device, namely the description of events 'from below'. Smiřický, although well-known, is a man of modest intellectual ambitions and of uneven education, but it is precisely these shortcomings that equip him with the ability to see things more realistically than some of his more 'distinguished' literary colleagues. Smiřický is a sort of intellectual Good Soldier Švejk, whose instincts of self-preservation ultimately turn out to have a greater moral worth than the misguided enthusiasm of the makers of the Prague Spring. His common-sense approach to life contrasts with the harebrained scheming of the frenzied reformists, who lost all sense of proportion and led the country into a disaster which was, in Smiřický's view, largely avoidable. The narrator forms the link between the various movements, levels and episodes of the novel. He is either an active participant in the events or an interlocutor with other narrators. Although the former case is by far the more prevalent, as a character Smiřický does not approach the importance his counterpart had in *The Cowards*.

The title of the novel is derived from a code name allegedly used by the secret police for a clandestine operation aimed at discrediting the Catholic Church. In 1949, the Church was regarded by the government as a potentially significant source of organised opposition. In *Miracle* the history of the clandestine operation is presented in the form of a crime novel. Škvorecký uses facts which surfaced during the Prague Spring, albeit with the interpretative licence of a fiction writer. In 1949, Father Doufal, a priest in a small parish in Bohemia, was accused of 'subversive activity', namely of having manufactured a fake miracle during the celebration of Mass in his church. The miracle, which was witnessed by scores of his parishioners, consisted of a suggestive movement of the statue of St Joseph on the main altar. According to the official account of the authorities who 'investigated' the miracle, the movement was produced by Doufal himself by means of a simple mechanism he had operated manually from his pulpit. This alleged fraud was used by the government as the pretext for a massive propaganda campaign intended to discredit the Catholic Church, a campaign that culminated in the crushing of clergy and prominent laity in a series of show trials.

The novel reconstructs these events and arrives at the conclusion that the miracle was actually staged by a special unit of the secret police, and that Doufal, who was subsequently tortured to death, had in fact taken no part whatsoever in the fraud. This finding, however, by no means ends the mystery. The inquiry, as developed in the novel, leads to another problem, which gradually assumes a greater importance than the police conspiracy. As it turns out, the police had originally planned to stage the phony miracle by installing a wireless-operated device under the statue of the Virgin after whom the church was named. However, all who were present at the church, as well as the official account of the miracle, had claimed that the statue of the Virgin remained motionless, and that only the statue of St Joseph had moved. The investigation is conducted during the Prague Spring by Juzl, a young journalist on the staff of a newly reinstated Catholic periodical. Smiřický himself is drawn into the inquiry: he had lived in the town in which the incident happened and was actually present during the fateful Mass. However, he did not actually witness the event with his own eyes since, bored by the ceremony, he had dozed off during the crucial minutes when the miracle had taken place. He is nevertheless keenly interested in this affair and provides Juzl with several useful tips. Occasionally, he even acts as a Dr Watson to Juzl's Holmes.

Juzl and other Catholic believers who aid in this investigation arrive at the conclusion that the discrepancy cannot be explained in any other way than as an instance of divine intervention: a faked miracle had turned into a real miracle. Smiřický agrees that, paradoxically, the theory of a miracle is the only plausible one but, being an agnostic and a sceptic, he cannot accept it. Thus the event remains enigmatic and by the end acquires a symbolic dimension. 'Life is a poorly structured detective story in which truth is the criminal but the detective is forever frustrated in his efforts to catch up with it', comments the narrator.[2] (p. 575) This aphorism underlies the philosophy of the entire novel. All values are relative; the human condition is essentially absurd. History is part of the relativistic universe, and the Czech experience, including the Prague Spring, ought to be seen from this point of view. The world is devoid of rational meaning, and irrational concepts, such as faith, moral principles and personal heroism are not viable.

The narrator's attitude to the absurd human situation is ambiguous. On occasion he is proud of his detachment and, like Dostoyevsky's Underground Man, but with much less spite, rejects all 'men of action'. On the other hand, he envies the believers' and even the fanatics' ability to be totally carried away by their dedication to an idea. The former sentiment is expressed, for example, in the following comment on the undying spirit of the Prague Spring even after the Warsaw Pact intervention: 'My feeling that I was the only sober person in a world populated by fools or inveterate drunkards, which haunted me during the entire period of the spring renaissance, has only increased after my return to the occupied land'. (p. 443) But a different sentiment permeates the following passage at the end of the novel, when the narrator surveys the history of his life: 'I remembered the martyred priest and I felt like crying. I am growing old, and getting sentimental, I told myself. But it wasn't old age. It was because I didn't understand. Because I lack faith. Faith in anything. Because I want to believe but can't, and I so badly want at least to be able to understand. *Quia absurdum. Quia turpe. Quia indignum.*' (p. 572)

The development of the narrative movement which centres on the miracle follows the pattern of a mystery novel in a rather loose fashion. It has its principal investigator, its surprises, red herrings, and other familiar elements, but in some ways it is an anti-mystery novel, a genre with which Škvorecký also experiments in *The Lion Cub* and in his exile detective stories. A typical tale of mystery consists of a stripping off of one illusion after another until the naked truth can be seen. *Miracle* follows the opposite course – the solution becomes more and more obfuscated by insoluble questions. Furthermore, the method of intertwining several narrative strands considerably reduces the elements of suspense. There are episodes belonging to the mystery movement which are separated by dozens of pages of narrative episodes which have nothing to do with the mystery.

The second principal narrative movement of the novel is pasted together from various episodes in the narrator's life. The focal point of this movement is Smiřický's love-affair with Věra Procházkova, nicknamed Foxy (Liška). Danny's acquaintance with Foxy goes back to 1949, the time of his brief career as a teacher in the School of Social Service. The girl, then only seventeen, was one of his students, and by using explicit, provocative advances she had seduced the young teacher who was the idol of the all-girl high school. After a year the affair ended because of Smiřický's call-up. Several years later, when Foxy was already a married woman, their affair resumed and she actually had a child by Smiřický, and, indeed by another man who was also not her husband. The narrative dealing with the events of 1949 is subsequently followed up only with sketchy information about the resumption of the affair.

Foxy, a shrewd but not particularly intelligent girl, is a blend of Lolita, a Hemingway heroine, and Dostoyevsky's repentant females, or, more accurately, a parody of all of them. The Danny-Foxy love story is narrated in an anecdotal manner, with the emphasis on the comic aspects of the story. Smiřický is only too eager to succumb to the overtures of the girl but, unfortunately for him, he had only shortly before contracted gonorrhoea from a young teacher of Russian, who in turn had contracted the disease from a Brazilian black. Because he does not want to disclose his problem to Foxy, he embarks on a delaying tactic by pretending that his religious beliefs prevent him from consummating the affair. The girl, who had never before been exposed to any religious sentiments whatsoever, is so impressed by Danny's renunciation that she herself becomes a convert. She is baptised and joins the Roman Catholic Church. Most of the early chapters of the novel consist in the comical scenes concerning these two profoundly sensual individuals who are frustrated in their desire for each other. This part of the novel manifests Škvorecký's method of threading one anecdotal episode into another at its best. There is not much of psychological interest in the relationship; instead the narrative technique relies on a robust, uninhibited humour that treats sexuality as a source of pleasure and entertainment. Even Foxy's conversion is treated as comedy rather than crisis.

The story reflects Škvorecký's paradoxical conception of Christianity; he tends to see Christianity as a complex interplay between the spiritual and the sensual, the sublime and the base. He has himself commented with studied, 'philosophical' frivolity on the intertwining of the motifs of venereal disease and religious conversion. In *Self-Dig-Book* he writes:

The motif of gonorrhoea is, I think, well conceived in *Miracle*. Our religious fathers used to tell us that the ways of the Lord were inscrutable. I used this idea as a point of departure for Foxy. After all, a heathen, she became a Christian only because her lover had contracted gonorrhoea during that critical time and because he was ashamed to tell her and so pretended to that sexual restraint which was required of Catholic youngsters. Foxy found this so incredible that she began to be interested in this strange religion . . . In spite of the fact that she later sinned in many ways – and who would not? After all, we know that even the Saints did and many times a day at that – she nevertheless took the winding path to God. At the beginning of the path Danny's bacteria are imported from Brazil. Isn't this the inscrutable path that leads to the Lord? . . . In Christianity I always liked the close proximity of the divine and the human, the saintly and the sinful, the beautiful and the ugly.[3]

The motif of the conversion has structural importance because it provides a link to the motif of the miracle. The priest who baptises Foxy is none other than Doufal, in whose parish the episode takes place. Doufal's simple, peasant-like world-view is a significant factor in Foxy's decision to join the Church. He becomes her spiritual mentor and turns Foxy into a regular church-goer. Danny, who is forced to go through the motions of belief, has to accompany her, much to his annoyance. They are both present at the Mass when the miracle occurs; only Foxy, however, sees the movement of the statue, since Danny is dozing off. Foxy provides a link between the narrative movements even in the latter parts of the novel, when she marries a member of the Catholic group of poets, who is himself deeply involved in the 1968 investigation of Doufal's death and of the twenty-year-old miracle.

Numerous other strands of action are attached to the Danny-Foxy love story. The most successful is the satirical portrayal of school during the first years of Stalinism in Czechoslovakia. Škvorecký introduces a gallery of characters directly or indirectly associated with the institution – teachers, local officials, members of the secret police, as well as ordinary citizens. Some are fanatics; others are careerists and opportunists, and still others are simple, honest people fighting for survival amidst the horrendous transformation of their lives, a transformation the scope of which they are not yet quite able to comprehend. The school becomes a microcosm of the country, with even the most trivial incidents acquiring a general political significance.

Among the more memorable characters is the teacher Milada, a fundamentalist Communist who has lost all sense of instinctive morality. The meaning of the character is somewhat diminished by Škvorecký's Freudian interpretation. Milada is to him not just a socio-political phenomenon which could have been found in Czechoslovakia by the millions during the Stalinist period, but also an old maid whose dogmatism is related to her sexual frustration. A foil to Milada is the principal of the school, Irena, an early Marxist reformist by intuition rather than by theoretical conviction. Her humanitarian values, combined with her ability to use quotations from Marxist literature to support her reformist arguments, exercise a significant restraining influence on the application of the dogma of relentless class struggle during the initial phase of the Revolution. Like so many other moderates who put their very livelihoods at stake during the Stalinist era, she remains unappreciated when reformism becomes the official line. During the Prague Spring, she is publicly accused of having had a destructive influence on her pupils during the Stalinist era, and she eventually commits suicide after the Warsaw Pact intervention of August 1968.

Some anecdotal episodes attached to the Danny-Foxy movement are successful, while others are less so. One such episode consists of a description of the graduation examination of the school by an outside state commission. Danny had had the ingenious idea of teaching the girls a simple set of Marxist formulae and their mechanical application to all possible aspects of knowledge. The examination turns out to be a great success, in spite of the fact that the girls, one after another, do little more than repeat Marxist clichés in slightly different sequences. This episode still works because of the narrator's satirical gift. Another anecdote, which is developed at considerable length, is, however, much less felicitous. It concerns Foxy's prank which consists of playing a game of chess by mail with a well-known Russian chess master. Having only an elementary knowledge of the game, she adopts the stratagem of simultaneously challenging the number one Czech chess master to a game by mail, and then uses the moves of both men against each other. The scheme works remarkably well at first, but finally the truth comes out and the matter is treated by the authorities not as a juvenile prank, but as a political provocation. The story reminds one to some degree of Milan Kundera's novel *The Joke*, which is also based on a silly prank that is turned into a political crime by a humourlessly imbecile régime. Škvorecký's story does not quite work, not only because of its extreme improbability, but also because one has difficulty in attributing such an elaborate intrigue to the one-dimensional shrewdness of Foxy.

The third, and from the thematic point of view the most important narrative movement, consists of loosely related scenes of political significance in which Smiřický acts as a narrator-observer. Some of the scenes are from the pre-Dubček era, but mostly they deal with the Prague Spring and events immediately following it. It was particularly this level of the novel that set off a heated controversy among Czech exiles and the intellectual underground in Škvorecký's homeland. The brief period of 'democracy' that evolved in Czechoslovakia in 1968 without any outside influence was without precedent in the Soviet Bloc. It came to be regarded by Czech patriots, despite its tragic end, as one of the finest hours in the country's history. In contrast to this almost universal view in the early 1970s, Škvorecký's novel is a biting, and in some places venomous, satire against the reform movement. The Communist reformists are in the eyes of Škvorecký either impractical romantics, or guilt-ridden neurotics, who in their need to cleanse their conscience from their participation in the disastrous twenty-year rule of Communism in Czechoslovakia, had embarked on the dangerous, irresponsible route of direct confrontation with Soviet power. The author extensively portrays the ideological hangover of the 'honest' Communist, but shows little sympathy for it. What is even more interesting, however, is that even the non-Communist participants in the Prague Spring are treated with considerable harshness. The liberal movement appears through Škvorecký's narrative lens as radicalism in reverse, rather than as a prudent, common-sense trend that might eliminate the vestiges of ideological excesses. The novel's account of 1968 is not historically reliable, nor does it pretend to be. History serves the author as the pretext for an unabashed political pamphlet. *Miracle* portrays the Prague Spring as a grotesque carnival of fools, a period of mass madness, during which only a few individuals, such as his narrative surrogate Smiřický, had preserved their sanity.

In his satirical account of the Prague Spring, Škvorecký uses deliberate ambiguity as regards fact and fiction. He is a master at creating suspense based on the reader's unsatisfied curiosity as far as the authenticity of characters and events is concerned. This curiosity is fanned by the author not only in the works themselves, but also in his comments on the works (especially in *Self-Dig Book*). In his earlier novels, the readers' curiosity is mostly limited to the autobiographical veracity of the adventures of the author's narrative surrogate. In *Miracle*, the situation is more complex. While the autobiographical interest is still present, the reader is even more interested in the historical authenticity of numerous events he witnesses through Smiřický's observations. At the time of the book's appearance, the degree of appreciation of the novel as a *roman à clef* varied. Some characters and events were easily identifiable by almost every educated Czechoslovak reader. Other characters and events were recognisable only to those with access to inside information. Still other characters and events appear not to have been based on facts at all. The search for parallels was in the 1970s a favourite game of Czech readers, which could not have been duplicated when the novel was read by foreigners who did not know the Czech literary situation, even though some of the characters in the novels were parodies of individuals well known in the West. For example, the Stalinist fanatic of the 1940s, Vrchcoláb, who is lampooned by Škvorecký after he becomes one of the pillars of the reform movement in the late 1960s, is transparently modelled on the playwright, novelist and poet, Pavel Kohout (presented under the name Vrchcolák in *The Tank Corps*), whose work has been extensively published and produced in the West. The other naive believer in the success of the reformist movement, Hejl, is a fictionalised version of Václav Havel, perhaps the Czech dramatist most respected in the West since Karel Čapek. Bukavec, the most comically pitiful character of the entire novel, who is ridden by insane guilt on account of his early involvement in the Communist movement, is Luděk Pachman, an internationally known chess master and political dissident of the late 1960s. More than a decade and a half after its publication, that aspect of the novel which constitutes a *roman à clef* has lost most of its meaning.

As far as specific government and party officials go, Škvorecký intentionally distorts their names and functions. Some historical figures are referred to by their correct names, like, for example, the two Communist Presidents, Gottwald and Zápotocký, but names of other individuals are quoted as if the narrator were suffering from partial amnesia. Thus the infamous minister of justice, Čepička ('little cap' in Czech) is transformed into Klobouček ('little hat'), the minister of information Kopecký is referred to as Kopečný, and so on. In the eyes of an informed reader, this device results in the diminishing of the historical significance of these figures. Phonetic alteration also occurs, however, with some 'positive' characters, albeit for different reasons. The name of the martyred Father Doufal is derived from Toufar, the modification of the name being probably motivated by the author's intent to imply the presence of the fictional element in his portrayal without severing the link to the character's life model. The representatives of the Party and government of 1968 are referred to exclusively by their titles rather than by their names. The leader of the reformist movement, Alexander Dubček, is not mentioned a single time by name in the novel. He is merely the First Secretary of the Communist Party. Another leader of the Prague Spring, Černík, is referred to only as Prime Minister, and so on. The use of the sometimes rather elaborate titles and attributes instead of names goes back to the era when the country was a part of the Austro-Hungarian Monarchy. By virtue of the association with the title-conscious pomposity of that era (which had never been entirely erased from Czech social habits), a subtle irony is created as regards the representatives of a 'socialist people's democracy'. Even those who are unfamiliar with the socio-historical background can easily perceive the deliberate grotesqueries in Škvorecký's portrayal of official circles.

The historical or quasi-historical movement of the novel has three strands. The most extensively used strands are the passages dealing with the activities of the Writers' Union, which played a dominant role in the Prague Spring and of which Danny, by virtue of his profession, is a member. The second strand consists of descriptions of government officials and is predominantly developed through his interaction with the activities of the members of the Writers' Union. The third strand is the narrator's observations of miscellaneous events during the Prague Spring: public gatherings, street corner scenes, as well as events that took place during the Soviet-led occupation.

The most effective parts of the novel are those which are set in the milieu of the Writers' Union. Škvorecký draws here upon his personal experience; this found its way into his work for the first time in *The Lion Cub*, but in *Miracle* he develops the portrayal of the *literati* on a broader scale. The author parades a variety of characters, impulsive enthusiasts, cynical nihilists, wavering opportunists, noisy braggarts, effete poets, petty schemers, as well as 'men of vision'. In spite of the variety, the overall impression of the Writers' Union is that of a strangely homogeneous group. The Union is perceived as a huge melting pot, which tends to reduce individuality by virtue of the special social privileges it provides. The author's dislike of this institution is evident; only a few individuals escape portrayal in a distorting mirror. The device of labelling by titles and attributes is used by Škvorecký profusely in the passages dealing with members of the Union. Thus Nabal always carries the attribute 'a talented prose writer', Očenáš 'author of science fiction', Hejl 'world-famous dramatist', Kocour 'permanent avantgardist', and so forth.

The satirical climax of the novel is reached in the description of a meeting of the Union during the heyday of the Prague Spring. It should be noted that for the purpose of highlighting the collapse of the Communist movement, the author uses throughout the novel the device of confronting the past (the Stalinist era, mainly the year 1949), with the present (Prague Spring, 1968). This device is developed principally in the form of the narrator's direct description of the behaviour of the radicals-turned-liberals. At the Writers' Union meeting, the method is taken to its cruellest limits. Škvorecký uses a ritual which was widely performed during the Stalinist age: the exposure of a 'class enemy' or of a 'residual bourgeois vice' at a public gathering. Such an exposure usually had damaging consequences for the person or persons accused, but sometimes, when the accusations were for lesser transgressions, the accused could escape punishment through 'self-criticism' and 'self-debasement'.

The ritual of self-debasement, an unconscious analogue of church confession, is described extensively in the part of the novel which deals with the School of Social Service in 1949. Individuals are made to confess their mistakes and denounce their class origin. At the Writers' Union meeting, the situation is reversed. Two individuals, former hardliners who actively participated in Stalinist excesses, are placed in the position of the accused by the new, liberal leadership of the Union. The two pilloried are Burdychová (whose ironic attribute is 'the sensitive chronicler of young girls' destinies'), probably based on the prose writer Marie Majerová, and Vohnout, allegedly based on the poet Ivan Skála, but appearing more like an amalgam of several individuals.

Burdychová is the quintessential naive 'liberal' intellectual with Communist leanings, who surrendered not only her reason but also her feelings to the authority of the Party. Her greatest intellectual crime was her fiery invective, published in the Party's official newspaper, against a group of her own comrades, who were accused of high treason during one of the Stalinist purges (the trial of Slánský et al.). Eleven of the accused were eventually executed, while others received long prison sentences. Burdychová's defence at the meeting is a parody confession of a disillusioned ex-believer, whose moral value, if not sincerity, is doubted by the narrator. The description of the pathetic scene comes to a climax in Burdychová's hysterial weeping, which the narrator conveys as follows: 'Again she pressed her handkerchief to her face, and as she was pressing it, a pink streak flowed down her chin. The handkerchief was of poor quality, and its colour ran'. (p. 138)

The pillorying of Vohnout is much more venomous. Unlike Burdychová, Vohnout is a quintessential opportunist who had built his career on perennial adjustments to changing political circumstances. He reminds us of Procházka in *The Lion Cub*, but lacks entirely the redeeming traits of that lewd editor. Vohnout's opportunism is parodied in the scene depicting his facing the torrential eloquence of his chief accuser. Vohnout, who before World War II had been a *Blut und Boden* ultra-conservative nationalist, became a Nazi sympathiser during the occupation. He translated the poems of Hans Carossa from German into Czech. After the war, he promptly joined the Communist Party, and, in his writings supported the Stalinist purges (compare, in real life, the poet Donát Šajner). Throughout the 1950s he belonged to the hard-line wing of the Party and wrote a scathing attack against Pasternak, whose work he had never read. However, in the 1960s, he turned for opportunistic reasons into a liberal, and became a translator of Pasternak's poetry. The reaction to the quoting of the verbal excesses of Stalinist journalism ascribed to Vohnout becomes in the context of the new era a surrealistic experience:

> I looked at the bearded faces of the experimental authors who were transformed into a painting by Giotto, into a crowd staring with innocent eyes at the substance of substances of a repugnant miracle. They listened to this authentic but now totally incredible text as if it were the roar of an awakened Godzilla, and I heard through it the sweet voice of a lovely woman talking from the abyss of unclean times, something like the voice of Gertrude Mendel, who went through two hells but remained alive nevertheless. (p. 132)

Finally the description reaches the physical dimensions of a Gogolian hyperbole. The youngest generation of *literati* become so outraged by the account that, in order to dramatise their rejection of the past, they destroy portraits of authors hanging on the meeting-room walls, among them the authors of some of the most distinguished nineteenth-century Czech classics.

The intertwining of motifs associated with the Stalinist era with those associated with the Prague Spring is not there merely for the sake of contrast. Nor does it occur only on the psychological level. Frequently the author alternates episodes from 1949 and 1968 just to create ironical analogies by implication. Thus chapter 6, entitled 'The Spring Farce', contains scenes from both periods. Ostensibly, the title refers to the farcical episode of the graduation examination at the School of Social Service, and simultaneously to the three-way chess game. But by implication the narrator wants to convey his negative interpretation of the euphoria of the Prague Spring. The episodes from both 'springs' are deliberately mingled.

To make this complicated part still more involved, Škvorecký injects yet another anecdote into the narrative flow, one of the best in the entire novel. It describes Danny's trip to Vienna, where he participates in an international convention on literature. The highlight of the trip is his meeting with Arasidov, a melancholic but eccentric Russian with a love-hate attitude to his country, the West and practically everything else. The anecdote is spiced by tabloid-like gossip about an incident which involves a KGB agent who is compromised by a friend of Danny's, who poses as a prostitute. This anecdote, which blends politics, literature, sex and pure slapstick with allegory, makes delightful reading.

The parts of the novel preceding the Soviet-led intervention of 21 August 1968 are clearly superior to the rest. After this event, Škvorecký's quasi-chronicle loses much of its uninhibited vitality. His humour becomes strained and self-conscious. Relatively most successful are the episodes that are least affected by political considerations, such as the story of the chase for a manuscript Danny had written during the liberal wave before the Soviet occupation and which, because of the rapidly changing atmosphere, becomes a serious liability for Danny's future. The retrieval of the manuscript from the publisher with the aid of Danny's friend, a convicted burglar, manifests Škvorecký's dark humour at its best. Another complication in this anecdote is provided by a promiscuous woman, who plots to get hold of the manuscript in order to use Danny for sexual purposes in the future.

The scenes describing the intervention and its aftermath are much less compelling. Škvorecký succeeds quite well when describing the foolhardy optimism of the diehard reformists, which persists even after the occupation. However, the narrative has an artificial ring, not to mention moments that are positively repugnant, such as Škvorecký's description of Jan Palach's self-immolation in protest against the presence of the Russians. The event, which has no precedent in Czech history, profoundly shook the nation, and the rest of the world, and in fact helped to delay the final takeover by the reactionary wing of the Communist Party. 'One day, on Wenceslas Square, some kind of student set himself on fire', comments the narrator. (p. 445) With the same uneasy levity, the narrator relates the apparent murder of Bukavec (Pachman) by the secret police. The occupation itself is recounted with some documentary accuracy, but Škvorecký's portrayal of the Soviet army is woefully stereotypical. The Russians are described as over-sexed, uninformed and under-educated, and in general become a laughing stock.

Among the weakest episodes are those describing Danny's experiences in the United States and Canada, whence he flees after the occupation. The portrayal of American society is essentially limited to a portrayal of the radical Left of the late 1960s and early 1970s, which for the narrator is substantially more repulsive than the radical Left of the East. In its intolerance of others, the American Left surpasses that of its Eastern counterpart. Thus Danny is unceremoniously ejected from a discussion meeting on Marxist philosophy by American intellectuals after he had dared to voice his dissent on certain points. The young people's anti-Vietnam War demonstrations are portrayed with open hostility and almost with sympathy for the riot police. The climax, a description of one such demonstration, ends in a Freudian snapshot of a middle-aged woman Danny knows, interpreting graphically her political activism as sexual frustration:

> The policeman, his face covered by a plastic visor, hit the broad over her head. ... Her pig-like squealing turned into a howling, and, bloodied but gratified, she fell on the ground of the square, kicking her fat legs towards the hot sun. Her micro-miniskirt rolled up over her waist, and through her transparent minipanties one could see the greedily bristly underbrush of her once active crotch. (p. 260)

The second part of the novel is furthermore burdened by artificial ideological disputes. The author introduces a functional character, Laura, an orthodox Czech Communist. Laura is a master of Marxist dialectics, and has ready answers to all Danny's arguments against the theory and practice of the Communist movement. However, in spite of her brilliance in debate the author implicitly always manages to compromise her views. Paradoxically, each argument won by her on the theoretical level discredits her ideology on the moral-pragmatic level. A parallel character to Laura is Bárta, an embodiment of Communist-style evil, a satanic brute of considerable intelligence, who appears as if from nowhere under the most unexpected circumstances, a mystical symbol of the indestructibility of evil. Another feature of the post-occupation narrative is a string of episodes involving the adventures of an Americanised Czech Jew, Kohn, who after thirty years had decided to visit his native country, only to be surprised by the occupation. Some episodes appear to be a spin-off from the short stories with Jewish themes Škvorecký had written a few years earlier.

No brief discussion of Škvorecký's novel can do full justice to all the characters that appear and disappear in various stages. Those who favour an instinctive life over one based on ideologies are described with obvious sympathy. The frivolous Foxy is declared by the author to be a 'positive' heroine of the novel, for example, and so is the hedonistic physician Gellen, whom Danny befriends during his gonorrhoea crisis. A practised seducer and a man of common sense, he is in some ways the narrator's alter ego. However, his comments on historical events are more philosophical than Danny's, and the author uses him frequently to expand on some of the principal narrator's observations. Another episodic hero is Lester, a promoter of jazz, which has an important value in all Škvorecký's works. The portraits of the unintellectual Communists also show sympathetic understanding. One of these is Ponykl, a low-ranking ex-member of the secret police, who chose his career as a result of his memories of the miserable life his parents had had during the Depression. Unlike when dealing with abstract situations, Škvorecký's sympathy clearly crosses political and ideological boundaries when he is portraying individuals. An endearing figure is the nun Udelina, who continues to perform her charitable work as a nurse without the slightest regard for the terror that is all around her. Her simple piety, like that of Doufal, is the subject of admiration and even envy on the part of the sceptical narrator.

Now, almost twenty years after its publication, the novel's emotional and intellectual imbalance is perhaps even more obvious than when it forced the reader to react to its deliberate satirical-polemical provocations. It is bewildering why Škvorecký needed to pillory the spirit of the Prague Spring so soon after its demise, though he has nothing to offer in its place. But it should not pass unnoticed that the book was written before the final crackdown on the vestiges of liberalism that came about only in 1972, a crackdown that turned Czechoslovakia into the most repressive country in the Communist Bloc with a near total displacement of a whole generation of the intellectual élite from public life. The unhappy fate of many of Škvorecký's friends would hardly have allowed him to portray the Prague Spring with the same comical abandon, if he had been writing a few years later.

On the other hand, Škvorecký's historical understanding of the Prague Spring remained essentially unaltered even in later years. On the occasion of the twentieth anniversary of the Warsaw Pact intervention, Škvorecký wrote for *The New York Times* an analysis of the Prague Spring in which he essentially repeats the theses set forth in *Miracle*.[4] According to him it was an ill-advised adventure led by guilt-ridden Communists and ex-Communists. Subsequent events in Eastern Europe have proved Škvorecký unjust. It became clear that the degree of tolerance on the part of the Kremlin leaders could not be reliably measured, and that the makers of the Prague Spring could not have foreseen the consequences of their efforts in 1968 any better than the liberal forces could in 1989 in Poland, Hungary, Czechoslovakia or even in the Soviet Union itself.

But Škvorecký's sentiments towards 1968 are probably more complex than he himself admits. Behind the self-indulgent façade of *Miracle* one also senses the author's despair over the disastrous outcome of the events. No doubt, the author's grimacing and clownish posturing masks the deep hurt that the fall of the liberal movement inflicted on his generation. When writing the novel, the destruction of patriotic, ideologically coloured sentimentality was perhaps also seen by him as an important task for Czechoslovak émigré society. There was perhaps a still broader reason that led Škvorecký to write his bizarre account of 1968. He probably saw himself as a spokesman of truth for its own sake, no matter how unpopular, a principle that has deep roots in Czech intellectual awareness, represented most eloquently in the teachings of T. G. Masaryk. Lastly, the novel's boisterous iconoclasm suited Škvorecký well as a unifying compositional device. It provided the novel with a distinct tone whose importance is especially well understood in those parts of the novel where the author makes little or no use of it. These parts are not among the novel's best.

6 The Swell Season

The novel *The Swell Season* (*Prima Sezóna*) written 1967–75, published in 1975 and translated into English in 1983, is a less ambitious work in the quasi-autobiographical cycle. Sandwiched between the monumental *Miracle* and *The Engineer*, it reads like a lighthearted intermezzo in the author's major fiction. Structured on the narrative of Danny, it repeats and extends some of the familiar situations from Škvorecký's earlier works, particularly *The Cowards*. Chronologically, the events of this work precede those of any of the other novels. They take place in the early 1940s, when Danny was a seventh-grader in the Kostelec high school, and the German occupation had not yet resulted in the serious disruption of the everyday life of Czech citizens. The Nazi presence is felt, but the atrocities have not yet reached the level at which people's conduct would be permeated by incessant fear. Only in the final episode are the later horrors intimated, when the news reaches Kostelec that the father of one of Danny's friends has been shot as a hostage. In all other episodes confrontation with German power is more fun than a threat.

The novel consists of six episodes that could easily be read as independent stories, covering a one-year period, the 'swell season' in the life of Danny. The principal theme of all of them is Danny's frantic but unsuccessful attempt to lose his virginity. When not chasing girls, he is preoccupied with playing jazz. Most of the characters are familiar. Danny's prime amorous object is once again Irena, but there is also Dagmar, Kristina, and Irena's sister Alena, as well as some twenty other belles, who are mentioned at least in passing. The author's stated objective was to write a *Silver Wind* of his generation. *Silver Wind* (*Stříbrný vítr*) is a novel by the Czech Fráňa Šrámek, written in 1910 and rewritten in 1921. It became a sort of profession of faith of the sensual world-view called Vitalism, which was particularly popular around World War I. However, Škvorecký's work differs greatly from Šrámek's. Škvorecký's sensuality is of a different kind, more controlled, and playful. Love and sex are to him more a game than a passion, and nowhere is this more obvious than in this novel. Virginity is a burden to Danny, but he is neither physically nor emotionally tormented by his inability to find a willing mate. Danny's own evaluation of his failure is free from hypochondria to a degree uncommon in an eighteen-year-old youth. The author develops the amorous intrigues, as he usually does, as comedy. His hero moves effortlessly from one girl to another, falling in love with each of them in his own superficially devoted way, and takes his lack of luck with good humour. Danny of *The Swell Season* is a much less complex individual than his counterpart in *The Cowards* and other novels.

The pattern of the six episodes is anecdotal. They all begin on a hopeful note, which tends to be strengthened in the course of the action. At the end, however, events turn against the protagonist. The stories all have pointed endings with an element of surprise. Danny's object of wooing either recoils, or consummation is disrupted by external circumstances, mostly in the form of parental interference. This pattern is established from the very outset of the work, so that the reader's curiosity is quite narrowly focused. Irena (who is much more capricious but also much more erotic than in *The Cowards*) is the elusive torturess in no fewer than three episodes. In the first episode, she unexpectedly encourages Danny to visit her at her home while her parents are away. As always with Danny, she retains full control of the situation, and permits him only a harmless necking session. But even this success comes to an abrupt end, since the couple fail to draw the curtains: their love-making is observed by Marie, another object of Danny's yearning, who, because she is jealous, makes an anonymous phone call to Irena's father. His prompt arrival not only puts an end to Danny's good fortune, but in addition exposes him to subtle humiliation from the shrewd man. In another episode, Irena takes Danny on a short mountain-climbing trip, but any possible intimacy between them is thwarted by an injury she sustains.

Irena's sister Alena is Danny's target in another episode. Jealous of her sister's success with boys, and as eager as Danny to get rid of her own burdensome virginity, she is willing to go 'all the way' with him. They go about it with all the thoroughness and ceremoniousness of the innocent and naive, which eventually becomes the cause of their undoing. They rent a hotel room in a nearby town, and the consummation of the affair appears to be imminent when the couple is betrayed by the hotel manager, who notifies Alena's father. Once again, the same man wrecks Danny's hopes.

All the stories are developed within the boundaries of playful probability, except the second. That story is structured on a fanciful plot that involves German twin sisters who are on a visit to Kostelec. They play a series of pranks on Danny, very much in the tradition of comedy of mistaken identity. This segment betrays the real purpose of the virginity theme in the work. Throughout, it is essentially used as a functional device for the sake of creating narrative possibilities rather than for the sake of psychological probing.

In comparison with Škvorecký's other novels, *The Swell Season* is two-dimensional, though it is refined and well choreographed entertainment. It is written with the light hand of an experienced narrator who does not fail to attract his reader's attention even during rather obvious passages, mainly because of his stylistic virtuosity. The blend of the Colloquial with the Literary language is perhaps more accomplished in this novel than in any of his other works. In spite of its theme, *The Swell Season*, by studiously avoiding vulgarity, possesses a crystalline, almost neo-classical elegance.

7 The Engineer of Human Souls

The Engineer of Human Souls (*Příběh inženýra lidských duší*) may be read as a sequel to Škvorecký's two other major novels, *The Cowards* and *Miracle*. The Czech version was published in 1977, while the English translation did not appear until 1984. It became an immediate critical success, particularly in the United States, where Czech émigré fiction had recently started to receive considerable attention. The title of the novel is an ironic reference to the notorious definition of a writer in Communist society according to the tenets of Stalinist aesthetics: the writer's work is expected to perform a propagandistic and didactic function. But the title also indirectly suggests the biographical or quasi-biographical nature of the novel, which is narrated in the first person by the author's surrogate, Danny Smiřický, who is already familiar to the reader from earlier works. The connection between the narrator and the author is implied in a number of ways. Like Škvorecký, Danny is an émigré Czech writer; he lives in Toronto and is employed as a professor of literature at Edanvale College whereas Škvorecký was at the time teaching in the same city at Erindale College. As in *Miracle*, an informed reader will find numerous parallels between the fictitious characters and authentic individuals, but the relationship between fact and fiction is of much less interest than in Škvorecký's previous novels. *The Engineer* is not a *roman à clef*, not even in the limited sense of *Miracle*.

The monumental novel, which, at 800 pages, is about two hundred pages longer than its immediate predecessor, *Miracle*, makes extensive use of some of the principal devices tested by Škvorecký in his earlier work. It is a polythematic, polyphonic composition which consists of loosely connected episodes and elements from various genres. The novel is developed in shifting chronological planes with flashbacks, flashforwards, flashbacks-within-flashbacks, narratives-within-narratives and digressions of all kinds. Characters appear, disappear and reappear. Some parts are written with considerable respect for historical authenticity, while others betray the author's insatiable '*Lust zu fabulieren*'. There are subtle observations on human nature, but extensive passages are written with an almost playful disregard for psychology, the probability of events, or even for narrative logic. The novel is full of surprises for even an experienced reader of Škvorecký's works. The stylistic cross-currents are so numerous and varied that on occasion one has the sensation of being overwhelmed by the sheer virtuosity of the author. The language includes passages written in high style as well as those saturated with colloquialisms, vulgarisms and dialect elements. Lengthy quotations in German, English, Russian and even Latin are also present. Structurally and thematically, the novel is still less cohesive than *Miracle*, which had at least some concrete formal boundaries – the probing of the 20-year-old mystery and the simultaneous political crisis of Czechoslovakia in 1968. *The Engineer* is almost provocatively shapeless and plotless.

On the other hand, as in *Miracle*, there are two temporal focal points between which the narrative shuffles back and forth – the 'present' (Smiřický's post-1968 life in exile) and the 'past' (his adolescence during the German occupation of Bohemia and Moravia in the mid-1940s). The episodes from Smiřický's émigré life are, with minor exceptions, set in Toronto, and those from his youth in the Czech provincial town, Kostelec. Events which took place during the intervening quarter-century are again given relatively little attention, although their influence on the destiny of the narrator, and of some other characters, are felt everywhere.

In comparison with *Miracle*, in *The Engineer* the role of the narrative *persona* is significantly enhanced. Not only does Smiřický attract much greater attention as a character, but also his intellectual level is raised substantially. While we still see many happenings 'from below', the new Smiřický is not just a practical, common-sense individual of limited intellectual ambition, but someone who does not hesitate to delve into the most abstract spheres. Rather than just an author of libretti for musicals and of detective stories, he is a writer of distinction. Moreover, he is a university professor. Škvorecký's surrogate advances views on a wide range of political, literary-critical and philosophical subjects. Indeed, there are passages in which the author uses him for outright sermonising, delivered with a self-indulgent air of superiority towards his 'inferior' cultural environment in the New World. Although not entirely incapable of regarding himself from an ironic perspective, the new Smiřický is a more self-assured and pompous person than his antecedents, and on occasion he is quite openly spiteful.

This quality applies only to the adult, the New World Smiřický. In the episodes from his youth in Bohemia, he is described quite differently from his émigré alter-ego. To a considerable degree, the young Danny resembles the immature, groping anti-hero of *The Cowards*. Some of the passages are so strongly reminiscent of Škvorecký's first work that it has been suggested that the author actually used leftovers from his early literary career. This is, however, unlikely. Many of the episodes from Kostelec in *The Engineer* are among the best prose Škvorecký has ever written, and their deliberate exclusion by the author from his first novel a quarter of a century earlier is hard to imagine. Moreover, upon close reading the Kostelec episodes from *The Engineer* tend to be less introspective, and there is a subtle difference in tone. The excursions into Danny's early life are overhung by a melancholy veil, as if the German occupation had become to the author more a source of nostalgia for his lost youth than a horrifying historical period. In spite of numerous repellent events, the fears and anxieties, the prevalent mood of the Kostelec episodes is of an almost childlike security. Many threatening situations have a happy outcome, and recollections of tragic events are coated with a veneer of lyrical sentimentality.

The world of Kostelec is populated with many characters recognisable from Škvorecký's earlier fiction. There are the numerous pals of Danny – Benno, Harýk, Přema and others; and the local belles – Irena, Dagmar, and Marie. However, some new characters play a substantially greater role. Three principal strands comprise the Kostelec narrative movement. First, Danny's involvement in an ill-fated sabotage scheme in the Messerschmidt fighter-plane factory where he is employed under the wartime emergency labour act (*Totaleinsatz*); second, his love story with Naďa, a sickly factory worker; and third, independent episodes structured mostly in an anecdotal form.

The sabotage theme is developed at considerable length, with numerous twists and suspenseful events which amount almost to a fully-fledged plot. The scheme consists of changing the specification of a small part in the machine gun with which the Messerschmidt fighter planes are equipped so that it becomes difficult, if not impossible, to use it. The scheme is soon discovered by the Nazi overseer of the factory, Uipelt, and Danny spends anxious moments in fear of imminent arrest. He even makes plans to seek asylum in a nearby monastery. However, the harebrained scheme does not result in any tragedy. As it turns out, the much-dreaded Uipelt, whose appearance is that of a model Nazi complete with a Hitler-like moustache, is in fact a member of the resistance, and he suppresses the whole affair. On top of that, he turns out to be a former American citizen, and an ex-member of the German-American Bund. He had emigrated to Germany in the 1930s, having naively believed in Hitler's promised land. Disillusioned by later developments, he became an active opponent of the regime. Danny's childish conspiracy almost compromises a much more important plan of the resistance, one that is aimed at slowing down the production of V-2 ballistic missiles. Uipelt takes a liking to Danny and even uses him for minor assignments in his underground activities – surely an unlikely proposition, considering Danny's demonstrable bungling immaturity. The jovial but powerful figure of Uipelt has the dimension of an archetypal saviour-protector. He is a variation of the mythical image of 'the Uncle from America', which is deeply imbedded in the subconscious of the citizen of the central European Old World.

Škvorecký has a strong disposition for inventing happy turns of events, but not necessarily happy endings. The modern fairy-tale-adventure-story turns into something quite different when Uipelt is captured by the Czechs after the end of the war. He is tortured and finally murdered by latter-day patriots before the characteristically vascillating and frightened Danny decides to make his move to save him. The senseless death of Uipelt is one of the many rallying points of the book's humanitarian appeal.

The sabotage motif is intertwined with the most captivating story from Danny's youth (*The Cowards* not excepted) – his love-affair with Naďa, a co-worker in the Messerschmidt factory. Of the numerous female characters in the novel, Naďa is the most important. Her importance is comparable to that of Irena in *The Cowards* or Foxy in *Miracle*. But unlike these somewhat shallow and frivolous females who played a major role in Smiřický's life, Naďa presents an idealised image of womanhood, almost a saintly figure – within the confines of Škvorecký's special understanding of human saintliness, one that regards sensuality as a virtue rather than a sin. Naďa is a poor peasant girl who became a factory worker to make a living, unlike Danny, who was drafted against his will. She is engaged to a member of her own class, Franta. She becomes Danny's lover mainly out of guilt for having instigated his involvement in the ill-fated sabotage, whose subsequent happy resolution nobody anticipates. However, the relationship becomes passionate on her part. Her spontaneity is so persuasive that her betrayal of her fiancé is never perceived as immoral; on the contrary, her feelings towards Danny are of exemplary purity. The affair with Naďa is Danny's sexual initiation. The psychology of the situation, however, is only marginally developed. In general, the episodes from Danny's youth explore sexuality much less than *The Cowards*. This shift is well within the novel's narrative logic, as the excursions into Danny's youth are seen through the prism of the recollections of the now middle-aged man, rather than an account of events from the immediate past, which was the stylistic illusion of *The Cowards*. The fact that the narrator speaks with two voices – one recounting the events as they happened, and the other editing them and commenting on them through a contemporary, often critical, vantage point – creates a different impact from *The Cowards*.

The love of Danny and Nad'a is complicated by their contrasting social backgrounds. Danny is a member of a prosperous, educated upper-middle class, while Nad'a comes from a family living in poverty. In spite of the war's tendency to democratise relationships between people, class distinctions never cease to influence their conduct. These distinctions manifest themselves in the different attitude towards both individuals on the part of the factory management, in the condescending remarks of Danny's friends, and in outright hostility on the part of Danny's mother. Although he tries to dismiss the problem as a meaningless prejudice, nonetheless he at all times feels the social gap between himself and his lover. The different background is manifested in her language which is replete in dialect elements, in her shabby, ill-fitting clothes which consist of pieces from male as well as female wardrobes, and in particular in her impulsive eating habits. As he soon understands, her attraction to food is not of the same kind as his own. It is not just appetite, but the genuine hunger of an underfed person. Nad'a's different background becomes obvious to Danny during her first visit at his home, when her conduct is a mixture of shy respect for unfamiliar luxury and an unconscious urge to take advantage of the situation:

> She explored our room with hungry eyes – the bronze chandelier with its crystal icicles and other marvellous things and her tiny nostrils were quivering beautifully. She was sniffing to see if there was something else to eat. 'Do you want more?' I asked. She nodded. I went to look into the kitchen and Nad'a followed me without invitation. My mother had left my dinner on the stove – horsemeat stew. Nad'a's nostrils quivered again. I lit the stove. 'It'll be ready in a minute', I said. 'Are your parents still alive?' 'My dad is, but he's in a concentration camp.' She looked around and

then she sat down on the stool by the stove. Class instinct, I say today in retrospect. A kitchen stool, the classic throne of Czech maids. But this did not occur to me then . . . . I put the whole serving of the stew on Naďa's plate – a substantial serving . . . and I watched with pleasure this bony girl devouring the horsemeat like a starving cat.[1] (I, pp. 30–1)

Curiously, Danny's feeling for Naďa is not one of superiority but of admiration, a phenomenon typical for Škvorecký's 'artificial' characters towards their 'natural' counterparts. Danny is aware that Naďa's mind operates on a lower level of sophistication than his, but he also understands that she has a set of values which, albeit over-simple, provides her with a self-assurance which he lacks. For Naďa, whose practical, realistic instinct as a member of the working class never abandons her, Danny is a source of temporary happiness. She idealises their relationship, but she is always aware that it will be of short duration. Her knowledge that Danny is ultimately inaccessible is perhaps paradoxically the very reason for her not feeling guilty for her infidelity. It is rather Danny who is on occasion overcome by guilt, both towards her and towards her fiancé, especially when he goes through typical Smiřický moments of scepticism towards the genuineness of his emotions. The motif of emotional sterility which pervades many pages of Škvorecký's previous works, most prominently in *The Cowards*, recurs, albeit mutedly, in *The Engineer* as well.

In spite of its realistic detail, the emotional superiority of the female character over her male counterpart suggests the romantic-sentimental pedigree of the story. The dénouement only reinforces this association. Naďa, as it turns out, suffers from tuberculosis, a fact she discovers only by accident. By then her condition is so critical that medical help is ineffective. She dies about a year after the war. She had married Franta, but died without having the children she had intensely longed for. Danny ignored her requests to visit her during the final months of her life, a failure that begins to haunt him as he grows older. The consumptive girl acquires an increasingly mythical dimension in the course of the narrative. More than just a character, she is a symbol of Smiřický's lost youth, and, more broadly, of the human being's habitual unpreparedness to recognise the true value of people and the true meaning of events until they are mere shadows of a memory.

From the narrative standpoint, the most extensively developed Kostelec episode in the novel is Danny's second involvement in anti-German activities, into which he is drawn by his friend Přema. A self-styled leader of a local group of young people, Přema single-handedly blows up a German fuel depot. Since he sustains slight wounds, he seeks out Danny, who has connections with a local physician. Škvorecký once again uses the situation for the examination of the relativity of heroism. On the one hand, Přema's daring deed is a noble act of patriotism; on the other, it has only a token influence on German military effectiveness, while reprisals against the local population are immediate. Several citizens (among them Danny's father) are arrested and sent to a concentration camp to discourage similar acts in the future. Seven of the hostages will never return. Is Přema's act to be viewed as folly or, in spite of its aftermath, a necessary contribution to the war effort on the part of the rather sheltered Czechs? The book's answer to this question is ambiguous.

The method of branching out a narrative stream delta-like into several strands, as employed in *Miracle*, is even more common in *The Engineer*. For example, Přema's sabotage story leads to another about the festering foot of Danny's father. Ever since World War I, when he was wounded while serving in the Austro-Hungarian Army, Danny's father has had a chronic infection. The foot requires frequent treatment, which becomes impossible after he is taken to prison as a hostage after Přema's act of sabotage. Following prison guards' complaints about the foot's odour, he is brought before a judge. It so happens that some quarter of a century earlier the judge had been his superior officer and had actually witnessed the infliction of the wound. The hearing becomes a reunion party and leads to the release of Danny's father from prison. Unexpected reunions – which sometimes appear to be closely modelled upon dramatic recognition scenes, and sometimes are more like their parodies – are common in Škvorecký's fiction. The author does not base the effect of these scenes on their credibility but on their playfulness, which tends to subdue or redeem otherwise grim chains of events. The story about the good fortune of Danny's father apparently ignores the fact that at that stage of the war, the Germans' administration of justice was outside the civilian judiciary. 'Life is terrible. And beautiful.' The dualistic homespun philosophy communicated via this unabashedly banal refrain, which recurs throughout the work, is translated into an 'anything-goes' narrative aesthetic.

Another outgrowth of the motif of Přema's sabotage is the introduction of Přema's father, Mr Skočdopole. Skočdopole belongs to a type frequently encountered in Škvorecký's fiction: an entertaining character in his own right as well as a narrator of enchanting, albeit to a degree apocryphal, stories. Skočdopole is a rabid nationalist who fought during World War I in the Czechoslovak legions, first on the side of the Russians against the Germans and then, after the October Revolution, on the side of the Whites against the Bolsheviks. Perennially under the influence of alcohol, Skočdopole is the source of a number of short narratives as well as of grotesque analyses of contemporary political problems. Despite the narrator's ironical attitude to this character, Skočdopole's analyses and predictions turn out to be surprisingly accurate.

The use of the lavatorial in the novel is abundant. The lavatory setting, which generates a humour (and pathos) of a Švejkian kind, is employed especially extensively, although not exclusively, in the Kostelec episodes. The choice of the setting is motivated realistically by the young factory workers' search for a temporary escape from their monotonous assembly-line routine. They use the huge lavatories as places for relaxation, gossip, fantasising about women, as well as arguing about political matters. The author employs the crude atmosphere of these gatherings to a degree which is occasionally sickening. As is typical of Škvorecký's narrative manner, the closed environment also becomes a convenient device for the unfolding of independent stories narrated by the temporary occupants of the lavatories. An entire cycle of more or less tall stories is developed by a factory worker who, because of his unusual complexion, is nicknamed the Green Man. According to himself, he had spent several months in Germany as a fireman positioned on an observation tower during the fiercest air raids. The Green Man's lavatory tales, each more fantastic than the last, though narrated with naturalistic detail, are received by his listeners with a mixture of appreciation, amusement and mock-angry protests. Each of the tall stories is different, yet their pattern is uniform. With the listeners' reaction equally predictable, gatherings featuring the Green Man are virtually ritualised. The ritualisation of narrative patterns and of secondary characters' conduct also occurs in other parts of the novel, for example in the scenes with the Toronto setting, featuring the Fat Man, as well as in later works by Škvorecký (for example, in *Scherzo Capriccioso*).

Scenes from Smiřický's émigré life occupy a larger part of the novel. Generally, they are of superior interest, since they contain a greater wealth of situations and characters. Yet none of the episodes matches the Danny-Naďa love story in poetic intensity. Smiřický's

The Engineer of Human Souls 71

career as a university teacher comprises the main narrative strand. The second, closely related to the first, is constituted by his love affair with one of his students, the beautiful and rich Irene Swensson. A third strand consists of miscellaneous, unconnected episodes. They deal mainly with the life of Czech émigré society in Canada, which Smiřický observes more than participates in.

The image of Evandale drawn by the author is that of a North American university of the 1970s. Škvorecký satirises the excesses of that period replete in political radicalism and fashionable educational experiments. Smiřický's colleagues are described as well-meaning and good-natured, but politically naive and preoccupied with problems that appear to Smiřický, with his central European historical experience, to be trivial and even bizarre. Smiřický's department parodies the experimental trends of the time. The classrooms are not equipped with chairs, but with plastic bubbles of various shapes that rest on wall-to-wall carpeting, so that students and their teacher appear like 'Gullivers between the bosoms of Brodnaga'. (I, p. 32) Moreover, to create a sensation of tranquility and womb-like security, a proposal has been made to suspend from the ceiling a canvas put together from surplus air force parachutes. Among numerous scenes lampooning college life, one in particular stands out. It describes the panicky reaction of the teachers to a report that one of their colleagues has just been attacked by his students during his lecture. They rush with security guards to his rescue, only to find that the class had merely been practising the principles of Artaud's theatre of cruelty. The bizarre episode has still more bizarre consequences, when the offended teacher files a grievance against his colleagues for their infringement of his and his students' academic freedom.

As a teacher of literature, Smiřický is put into a position whose paradoxical nature he is constantly aware of. By temperament non-academic, he has to perform tasks which require not just sensitivity towards the subject he teaches, which he has aplenty, but also systematic presentation and discipline. His experience as an author, his instinctive insight into literary works, as well as his broad knowledge, fail to win his students over. He is, with the exception of isolated moments, not an inspiring teacher who could retain his audience's interest. His pupils listen to him without concentration and perform their assignments in a routine manner. They cheat whenever they can. Smiřický, in turn, has become accustomed to their attitude. His students are made to read lengthy term papers aloud in class so that he can kill lecture time. He pays only perfunctory attention to their presentations. To spend as little time as possible on preparation, he uses identical material in courses with different titles. On occasion, he indulges in a sadistic display of power, as when he catches a careless plagiarist red-handed. But he does not take his occupation seriously enough to harm anybody. Sometimes, when a student's performance is particularly dismal, he even discreetly suggests the use of the underground term-paper service.

His students are generally an amiable lot, although as a group they are pitifully ignorant of basic political, historical, and even geographical facts. Their approach to literature is devoid of instinctive appreciation. They come from various ethnic backgrounds. The greatest attention, besides that lavished on Irene Swensson, is given to Hakim, a US citizen of Middle Eastern extraction, who had fled to Canada during the Vietnam War to avoid the draft. An exponent of a Marxist world-view, Hakim is something of an ideological antagonist to Smiřický. The author uses him primarily as a target of his own anti-Communist rhetoric. Unfortunately, the polemic is generally on a rather low level, since Hakim is basically an uneducated fanatic and no match for Smiřický's extraordinary expertise on Marxism. As in *Miracle*, the invectives against Communism are the weakest part of the novel, and sometimes make for painful reading. The character of Hakim is saved from absurdity only by the narrator's gradual softening of his attitude towards him. Smiřický ultimately becomes fond of him, preferring his passionate, albeit primitive, faith to the apathy of most of the other students. 'Hakim has once again had his say, a familiar old mixture of contempt, doubts, and hatred – and, at the same time, there is something that attracts me to him. We are members of a strange élite. We are concerned about things which other people are not concerned about.' (II, p. 207)

What primarily emerges from Smiřický's contact with the university world is a sense of isolation. There is little common ground between him and teachers or students. The barrier has been formed by an altogether different historical experience. Twentieth-century North America has never seen war on its soil, and knows Nazism only from secondhand accounts; Communist oppression is only an esoteric concept for which no true parallels can be found in the United States or Canada. Smiřický regards Canadians as 'children of the prairies' who are blessed by the absence of the major adversities that had helped to mould his own life. Precisely because of this privilege, they are deprived of an understanding of modern life's essential problems.

The Engineer of Human Souls 73

Indeed, as Smiřický concludes, they are deprived of an understanding of art and literature.

Škvorecký uses an elaborate compositional device to develop this leading theme of the novel, a device which is also used for the introduction and unification of other themes. He divides the novel into seven parts, each of them bearing a title of one American or English author: Poe, Hawthorne, Twain, Crane, Fitzgerald, Conrad and Lovecraft. The authors are the subjects of discussions in Smiřický's literature course; this provides a structural framework of sorts for the individual chapters. The work of each author is used for creating various compositional links with the narrative movements. Usually the psychology of the narrator, his subjective associations with the author under discussion, are the points of departure for achieving this effect. A passage from a book or a comment on it by his students may touch off a chain reaction in Smiřický's mind that frequently evokes memories of his past. It may also serve as an impulse towards a more intellectual reaction, which is elaborated in the form of a commentary addressed to his students, or else merely leads to an interior monologue or a thought. However, the narrator is frequently also associated with the literary material indirectly, by implication, through thematic or ideational parallels. The method is by no means consistently applied, since Škvorecký is not a writer who is either interested in or perhaps capable of creating a tight structural design. Frequently, a discussion of one of the particular author's works constitutes just another episode among many, and the chapter bears only a token relationship to the theme suggested in its title.

Some comments on a particular author make for literary criticism skilfully incorporated into a fictional context. One critic goes as far as to praise this aspect of *The Engineer*, calling it 'literary criticism of rare elegance, originality and intelligence'.[2] This claim is somewhat misleading. The critical passages are mostly impressionistic 'asides', and their originality and validity are debatable. Even the narrator knows better when he comments on his interpretations: 'Do I myself take my delirium seriously? Conrad's delirium? For such art is delirium. Such an author is a sounding board against which the forces of a bloody experience resound. The forces of visions, forebodings, the irrational power of art'. (II, p. 285) Perhaps appropriately, the literary-critical parts of the novel gain their full effectiveness only within the narrative context.

The most felicitous application of the method of using a particular author's work as a starting point for the development of multiple thematic strands can be found in the first chapter. The discussion of Poe's poems generates a wealth of narrative material, ideas and moods. The analysis of 'The Raven' creates an effective setting for nostalgic recollections of Smiřický's youth in Kostelec, with his brief love-affair with the consumptive Naďa creating a parallel for Poe's lost maiden. Smiřický's erotic speculations about Irene Swensson, who participates in the discussion, create a mundane counterpoint. The second theme the discussion of 'The Raven' develops has broad socio-cultural implications. To make his lecture more interesting, Smiřický has brought a Russian adaptation of Poe's poem by Yesenin–Volpin, which has a striking political message. Creating a serious parody of the original poem, the Russian poet used the structure, with its refrain 'Nevermore', to express his despair at the suppression of freedom in his country in the 1920s and his lack of hope for the return of better times. Smiřický first reads the poem to his non-Russian-speaking audience in the original and only afterwards in translation. He immediately feels, however, that the translation has destroyed everything. In this way, the chapter reinforces the pervasive theme of the novel – Smiřický's isolation as an émigré author, an isolation which results from linguistic, historical and geographical barriers. Škvorecký extracts yet another point from the discussion of Poe by indulging in a polemic against one particular interpreter of the poet, J. W. Crutch, who had commented that 'The Raven' possessed 'an almost brilliant perspicacity without demanding any actual experience of life whatsoever'. (I, p. 22) Smiřický rejects this interpretation: 'I could still hear the Russian verse rumbling in my ears, interpreting Edgar Allan Poe with immeasurably greater understanding than this literary critic possesses in spite of the long century and the ocean between them'. (I, p. 20)

The implications of Škvorecký's approach to literature, as set forth in this and other parts of the novel, are not without unintended irony. It is difficult not to notice that Škvorecký, in his emphasis on the topical relevance of literary works of the past, unconsciously becomes a victim of the pop aesthetics of the late sixties and early seventies, which on other occasions he ridicules. The idea of viewing a work of art from another era through the prism of present-day socio-political experience occurs again in the discussions of all the authors in subsequent chapters. In the chapter 'Hawthorne', a passage from *The Scarlet Letter* describing Dimmesdale's inability to release himself from the security of the dogma of his church is used to elucidate the power of Communist orthodoxy. Introduced by quotations from

Hawthorne, the passage culminates in a near-Surrealist vision of the other side of puritanism, the lavishly ceremonious customs of those in power: 'Stalin's bathroom, a bathtub of alabaster-like whiteness, and there are three gold taps opening into it. And they are celebrated in the daily press: one is for cold water, the other for hot, and the third for a perfumed water, everything for Stalin . . . I see Stalin naked, he is splashing himself in the bathtub with the perfumed water . . . Oh, Hawthorne, do you really know what you have written?' (I, p. 160)

The topical approach is taken almost *ad absurdum* in the chapter entitled 'Conrad'. This chapter contains a classroom discussion of Conrad's early novel set in Africa, *Heart of Darkness*. The students advance current academic socio-historical, biographical and Freudian interpretations of the protagonist, Kurtz, which they have lifted from secondary texts. Smiřický stuns his class by submitting that the story is actually a prophetic vision of the fate of Marxist doctrine after the Bolshevik Revolution. He supports his interpretation by the analysis of Harlequin, a weird disciple of Kurtz's, who is of Russian origin. The *New York Times* critic of Škvorecký recommended this interpretation as indispensable to anyone interested in Conrad. However, the originality of the passage is limited. The view that *Heart of Darkness* anticipates the modern cultural crisis of utopian visions turned sour had been voiced long before Škvorecký, and his interpretation of the role of Harlequin in the novel is artificial.

Other chapters are more modest in their ideological implications. 'Crane' is used to expand further the irreconcilable differences between Smiřický and his students. While the students regard the main theme of *The Red Badge of Courage* to be the initiation of a boy into manhood, with the Civil War acting merely as a naturalistic backdrop, for Smiřický the war is of central significance. The novel revives his memories of World War II with all its horrors, including the death of his friend who attempted to destroy a German tank (a story already used in *The Cowards*). Smiřický summarises his frustration thus: 'It doesn't make any sense. It is not Higgins's fault that there was no Gestapo in Canada . . . I am confronted with a classic situation. An attitude shaped by experience and by the reading of many sources is faced with a mind shaped by the atmosphere of the time and its television'. (I, p. 301)

Not much use is made of Fitzgerald in the chapter to which he lends his name, beyond a parallel between Irene and Nicole, the heroine of *Tender is the Night*. (In Smiřický's interior monologues Irene is usually called Nicole.) However, the parallel is largely limited to the similar social status of the two women. The proposition that Smiřický's fate might be analogous to that of Dick Diver is suggested only humorously. In 'Twain' and 'Lovecraft', the use of literary models is decorative rather than interpretative.

The Smiřický-Irene Swensson love affair seems to have been deliberately plotted as a foil to Smiřický's affair with Naďa. The two females are strikingly different. Naďa is an underprivileged, sickly girl, while Irene is a member of the upper class and in perfect health. In order to dramatise the contrast, Škvorecký seems to repeat some of the leading motifs in reverse. Irene's extravagant dressing habits are given as much attention as the shabbiness of Naďa. Irene's sealskin coat, patent leather boots, sophisticated dresses, her Vidal Sassoon hairdo, and meticulously made-up face, are essential details of her portrait. She drives a Cadillac and has free access to her father's yacht, on which she cruises the Great Lakes region. Irene's 'cover-girl' appearance is somewhat unlikely. In the early 1970s a girl with Irene's habits would have been laughed off a North American college campus.

The difference between the two females is not limited to their appearance or their social status; it is also reflected in the attitudes of the narrator. While Naďa was Danny's initiation into sex, an experience of a sensation-hungry youth, the liaison with Irene is the carefully controlled adventure of a sophisticated middle-aged man, whose sexual habits have been tempered by countless affairs. Furthermore, Irene is a virgin. Smiřický never allows Irene to become a threat to him, and deliberately maintains a teacher-pupil distance between them. He has only a casual sympathy for her infatuation and never develops any genuine affection for her. He makes her his mistress only after he has repeatedly humiliated her by haughty rejections. In spite of her warm nature, Smiřický regards Irene as too synthetic an individual, someone whose personality had been shaped by technological progress, television, movies, magazines, and a mechanical absorption of such shoddy pseudo-educational materials as sex manuals. The bizarre setting in which the consummation of the affair takes place (a car equipped with the most advanced gadgetry imaginable, reminiscent of James Bond movies) epitomises the narrator's ironic, detached treatment of the character:

> She threw herself against my chest with her Vidal Sassoon hairdo, almost knocking out one of my teeth . . . I put my hand under her tartan skirt. Over her blond hair I saw her reaching for the control

The Engineer of Human Souls 77

panel, and without looking, with the virtuosity of a piano player, she pressed one of the many buttons. For a second I had a feeling that some mechanical joke would take place – the roof of the convertible would go up and rain start pouring in. But she was born in a car. The broad back of the seat slowly started to descend. A genuine double bed was being created . . . Nicole loses her virginity in style, in an automobile. (II, p. 246)

Outside the academic world, the portrayal of native Canadians is limited to a small circle consisting of the Swensson family and their friends. The Czech émigré population is, however, richly represented. Once again Škvorecký moves between various modes – psychological, sociological, satirical and downright farcical. The stylistic diversity is facilitated by the narrator's changeable and ambivalent disposition towards his compatriots. They are a heterogeneous lot. The older immigrants do not get along well with the post-1968 immigrants. They particularly mistrust the ex-Communists, not being able to comprehend that during the decade preceding the 1968 crisis, the distinction between Communist and non-Communist had essentially lost its former meaning. The community is riddled with informers, and on occasion secret agents from Prague are sent to Canada on special, ostensibly absurd, missions. Smiřický considers himself a member of the émigré community, and yet he develops sufficient distance from it to take an ironic stance towards many aspects of its life. He shares with others nostalgia for their native country, but understands that it is essentially futile to maintain ethnic traditions in a distant foreign land. The frequent mass gatherings of the émigré community receive satirical treatment. Children sing patriotic songs, in Czech distinctly affected by a foreign accent. Particularly clownish are the meetings of old-timers, many of whom had arrived in Canada before World War II. Their sentimental hero continues to be the founder of the Republic and its first president, T. G. Masaryk. At one such meeting, a rare recording of a forty-year-old radio broadcast is to be played in commemoration of the long-dead president. Accidentally, that recording is confused with another, and instead of the solemn voice of Masaryk, the meeting hall is flooded with the grotesque falsetto of Mickey Mouse. Farcical, slapstick twists like this occur frequently in the novel. The satire of *The Engineer* is much more benign than that of *Miracle*, but many devices used by the author are identical.

The narrator, however, is profoundly compassionate towards many individuals in the émigré community. From among the host of characters of the immigrant population, the most fully developed is a young woman, Veronika Prst. This surname (meaning 'finger') is not common in Czech. It was apparently chosen by the author because it is difficult for a native Canadian to pronounce, since English, unlike some Slavonic languages, does not contain words consisting solely of consonant clusters. This phonetic peculiarity, together with the name's meaning, symbolises the tragi-comic isolation of this character. With no other character does Škvorecký make such a concentrated effort to dramatise the emotional and intellectual contradictions of an exile. Apart from Naďa, Veronika is the most vividly portrayed female character in the novel, despite the fact that she appears only in a small number of episodes.

Veronika is a former rock singer who had used the opportunity of a trip to the West to defect. In spite of her talent, she cannot find employment; her foreign accent is a significant liability in rock. Her real plight, however, is not economic but psychological. Being used to a life of danger, albeit one that also had a purpose, she is unable to adjust to the luxury of peace and freedom. Without tension and without a collective sense of purpose, life in her new country appears sterile and vacuous to her. While most others are capable of either suppressing or resolving their inner problems by compromises, Veronika is incapable of simple solutions. The ideal situation for her would be a life of freedom in her native country. But political realities impose a different alternative: it is either freedom and life abroad, or repression and life at home. At the beginning of the novel she opts for the former, at the end for the latter. She returns to Prague, although she faces recrimination and the status of an unreliable citizen. The fate of Veronika is raised to a symbolic level. She is doomed to be an outcast by heredity (the daughter of a Jew) as well as by socio-historical developments (Dubček's orphan). She is a 'child of the twentieth-century myth', comments the author. (II, p. 129)

The inclusion of Veronika in the novel is plotted somewhat conventionally in the form of her love-affair with Irene Swensson's brother, Percy. He is a sensitive, generous and straightforward young man, and his love for Veronika is genuine. He attempts to help her to overcome her sense of purposelessness by involving her in the civil-rights movement in which he himself is active. However, his efforts are futile, as Veronika finds the pursuits of the movement trivial in comparison with those behind the Iron Curtain. By the same token, Percy does not understand Veronika's past and regards her political and social views as narrow-minded and reactionary. The different cultural backgrounds rise as a barrier that neither good will, love nor physical attraction can overcome. The gap between them is manifested in ever sharper disputes, which comprise a blend of mutual accusations and guilt towards each other.

The most compelling scene featuring Veronika comes early in the novel. It describes her attempt to fight loneliness by playing Czech protest songs, even in the knowledge that the Canadian natives cannot understand them. So she plays them through the college tannoy system, but long after the lectures have ended. Her solipsistic performance is witnessed only by Smiřický and a few maintenance workers, who are cleaning the empty hallways.

Veronika's foil is another Czech girl nicknamed Stupe (Blběnka) who is a model of adaptability and assimilation. She has few ideals or scruples; her goal is security and material prosperity. Lacking any particular talent, she makes sexuality her main tool for the achievement of her objectives. By marrying a Canadian hippie, who happened to be on an East European tour, she had emigrated from Czechoslovakia with the permission of the government, not illegally as most members of the Czech émigré community had. After their arrival in Canada, she had promptly divorced him to search for a more desirable mate. Not particularly beautiful, she based her behaviour on appealing to men's erotic fantasies. Her clothes, speech and movements are calculatedly sensual, and border on vulgarity. This enables her to attract instant attention from men, but once contact is established, she adjusts her behaviour to a more decent level, which in fact corresponds more closely to her true personality. Stupe's strategy turns out to be successful since she marries a wealthy Canadian manufacturer and real-estate owner. Unlike Veronika's attitude towards her native country, Stupe's is devoid of tragic feelings. Being a legal émigré, she is allowed to visit Czechoslovakia regularly. She does not go there for sentimental reasons, or, more accurately, she goes for perverted sentimental reasons. Chiefly she wants to show off to her former friends and relatives how well she has succeeded in the New World.

Many other Czechs populate the pages of the novel. Some appear only once, some repeatedly. They include idealists and materialists, right-wing radicals and left-wing radicals, tragic characters and buffoons, crooks and saints. Of some greater interest is, for example, Smiřický's mistress, Margit. A nurse, she has an impeccable appearance and a peculiar set of principles. Married to a paraplegic, she has been maintaining an affair with Smiřický for years. They have both become accustomed to regard the relationship as purely serving biological needs, and as being therefore exempt from moral concerns. Margit is in reality a highly principled individual who uses Smiřický as a prophylactic device against the temptation of having affairs with other men. Margit's husband, Bočár, is a man cursed by fate. He spent years in a Communist prison, while Margit was faithfully waiting for his release. After their emigration to Canada, Bočár became a security guard. During the performance of his duty, he was shot and made an invalid for life. Bočár also serves the function of a narrator of stories from prison life. Another ex-prisoner is Pohorský, who had appeared for the first time in *Miracle*. Pohorský is a comic character, perennially preoccupied with harebrained plots against the Communist government in Prague. His schemes include a saturation radio campaign to mobilise American public opinion for the Czechoslovak cause, a chain letter urging the population of Czechoslovakia to buy as many boxes of matches as they could and thus create an economic crisis, letter bombs, and so forth.

An important place is occupied by some forty letters that appear in various parts of the novel. They are addressed to Smiřický by friends from his youth. The only exception are those of the Canadian Communist Booker, whose correspondence consists of comically naive statements addressed to his bride-to-be in Prague. The letters differ in number and in volume – Přema, Jan and Vráťa (eight letters each), Lojza (seven), Rebekka (five), Booker (four), and Naďa (one). It is characteristic for the function of the letters that the key character from Smiřický's past, Naďa, is the author of only one letter, and her émigré-life counterpart, Irene Swensson, of none. These characters are sufficiently developed through direct and indirect description that the author did not need to use the letter form. Přema is one of the more important characters from Smiřický's past. His letters are used to convey information on his later life. Other principal correspondents with Smiřický, Jan, Vráťa and Lojza, do not appear in the narrative at all, and Rebekka and Booker each appear in only one episode. Apart from being a device for providing information about familiar characters, and for the sake of introducing new ones, the letters serve as a polyphonic commentary on the changing times. The commentaries vary from the sophisticated to the over-simple, from descriptions of personal reactions to events to broad analyses of those events. Their mood varies from the sombre to the comic.

Přema's letters occupy the place of greatest importance in the novel. As a character, Přema is developed in great detail and his life is followed from boyhood to his premature death. The novel depicts him during the war as a genuinely heroic individual. As the narrative continues, he becomes one of the most moving characters of the novel, an individual who by circumstances and temperament is always in conflict with historical developments. The letters provide information about Přema after the Communist takeover in 1948, when he disappears from Smiřický's sight. Predictably, he joins the underground resistance. However, his anti-Communist activities do not go beyond the distribution of ineffective leaflets and senseless communications with agents abroad. His meaningless, wasted life continues after he flees the country. He is recruited into the French Foreign Legion, and spends six months in a training camp in the Sahara. Assigned to fight in Vietnam, he deserts the Legion, and is eventually placed in a camp for stateless persons in Sicily. Ironically, the most numerous inhabitants of the camp are former SS and pro-Nazi collaborators from various parts of Europe. Přema thus becomes a companion of those whom he had been fighting against several years earlier. His hopes to emigrate to America are dashed as he is found unsuitable because of his bad teeth. He finally emigrates to Australia, where he first works as a labourer, but later acquires, very cheaply, a farm. While at first he finds farming satisfying, he is incapable of coping with the loneliness of the vast underpopulated Australian bush. He returns to Sydney to manual labour. His letters to Danny from that period become fuller and fuller of nostalgia for his native country and the town of their youth, Kostelec. History has one more cruel joke for Přema up her sleeve. In 1968, during the heyday of the Prague Spring, after the general amnesty, Přema decides to return to Czechoslovakia. However, when he arrives in Prague, the country is already occupied by the Soviets and his friend Smiřický has in the meantime gone abroad. After a year, when re-Stalinisation is being consolidated, Přema is expelled from Czechoslovakia and returns to Australia. The last letter is not from him, but from the postmaster of the town where he had settled, informing Smiřický of his friend's accidental death.

While Přema's destiny might be found somewhat artificially constructed, he is, nevertheless, one of the most compelling male characters in the novel. He is a quintessential romantic, whose ideals are pulverised by the merciless reality of the twentieth century. At the end of his life, most of his enthusiastic urge for a full, committed life is all but consumed. His return to Czechoslovakia is in part motivated by practical considerations: free medical care in this socialist country, an important asset for this ailing man. While Přema is an eternal wanderer, Lojza is at home everywhere. While Přema is an idealist and adventurer, whose principles constantly draw him into conflict with his surroundings, Lojza is a naive materialist and a conformist. Like many members of the working class in Škvorecký's works, Lojza is not treated favourably. During the German occupation, he is easily won over by pseudo-socialist manipulation, such as the lure of formerly luxurious resorts, made available to 'deserving' workers. He even volunteers for work in Germany, and when the massive Allied air-raids begin, his letters reflect the official propaganda, complaining bitterly of the harm inflicted on the innocent German population. After the war, he marries a distant relative in Slovakia and obtains a farm as her dowry. Communist collectivisation is at first opposed by him since it threatens his property. However, once collectivisation is completed, he becomes an ardent advocate of the new system. Lojza's ideological somersaults are amusing rather than disturbing or offensive. There is much good-natured naïveté in him, and one never doubts his total sincerity. His spiritual life revolves around movies, which he judges according to the degree of female beauty displayed in them. In Lojza, Škvorecký has created a caricature of the modern happy man. Such an individual is only possible when he has the intelligence of a primitive being on the verge of idiocy.

While Přema and Lojza are men of action, the other duo of letter writers, Jan and Vráťa, are men of reflection. Like the previous two they are contrasting types, albeit both are intellectuals, Jan a poet, and Vráťa a playwright. Their correspondence, which covers almost a quarter of a century, reveals their unending conflict with those in power. Jan's reaction to changing historical circumstances is always accompanied by a painful inner crisis, a tendency that comes to a climax in 1968, when he commits suicide. Vráťa, on the other hand, a Czech in the tradition of Švejk, is capable of laughing off even the most shattering experiences. Jan is a typical left-wing intellectual, whose life-long error is that he believes that Marxism and humanism can find common ground, that the dignity of an individual can be preserved within the framework of a socialist state. He fails to comprehend that the historical course of Marxism has been such as to make the return to its original objectives impossible. His letters are a vicious circle of hope and depression that reflect the periodic changes in official policies. Jan represents a significant part of the Czech intelligentsia which, after World War II, was carried away by the ideas of the Revolution, only to discover that it had been corrupted by brutish power, and that its once brilliant intellectual vitality had degenerated into the bureaucratic rule of primitive minds. Jan's letters frequently have the character of essays. Jan is no doubt often used by the author as his mouthpiece. The originality of Jan's observations is uneven. The discussion of the similarity between Nazi aesthetics and Socialist Realism says little more than the obvious. On the other hand, the frequent comments on literary matters, such as the poets S. K. Neumann, Kolář and Holan, contain some critically valid points. Somewhat surprising is the denunciation of the literary critics of the 1960s, who are accused of negativism and intolerance.

Vráťa appears to be modelled on Škvorecký's friend, the playwright Vratislav Blažek. His letters suggest an extrovert, vivacious, indeed Harlequinesque, personality. They contrast sharply with the melancholy, brooding, self-doubting and almost masochistic mood that is typical of Jan's letters. However, behind this superficial difference, a life story with a similar pattern is unfolded. Vráťa, who had joined the Party after World War II, soon discovered the discrepancy between the ideal and reality. He tried to use his literary talents to write satirical allegories, pillorying corruption, but instead of reaping gratitude for his effort, he was sent to the coal mines for re-education. Thanks to his resilience, he eventually attained privileged status in Communist society, by becoming a scriptwriter and an occasional playwright. Since he had earned himself the reputation of a reformist, after Dubček's fall in 1968 he was blacklisted, and defected to West Germany, where he made a living as a scriptwriter for pornographic movies. The biographical aspect of Vráťa's letters is of secondary importance. Their primary interest lies in the extensive digressions, puns, anecdotes and satirical portraits of officialdom. Particularly elaborate is Vráťa's satirical treatment of Škvorecký's favourite target, the poet, playwright and novelist Pavel Kohout, who once again appears under the alias Vrchcoláb. The peculiar, almost overbearing humour that dominates Vráťa's correspondence has some absurdist touches. The language is deliberately distorted by ungrammatical phrases, misspellings, neologisms and verbal twists of many kinds. Ultimately, one gains the impression that one is witnessing the confession of a compulsive exhibitionist who is on the run from himself, of someone who has become so accustomed to wearing a clown's garb that it has become indivisible from his personality. The socio-political causes for Vráťa's personality are made, at least in part, quite unmistakable. Vráťa, the Harlequin, is as much a product of his time as Jan, the Pierrot.

The forty-one letters are a stylistic *tour de force*. Their psychological, social and thematic diversity are effectively transformed into a linguistic experience. For example, the temporary Germanisation of Lojza, and his later Slovakisation through marriage, are made concrete by the intrusion into his original modes of expression of new linguistic elements (lexical, phonetic and morphological). The reader not only understands Lojza's adaptability from the semantic context, but also senses it through his language. The technique goes beyond the probable, creating a hyperbolised stylistic effect reminiscent of Ionesco's plays.

Like every serious work of art, *The Engineer* elicits an emotional response which is not just the sum total of its individual parts. Škvorecký subtitled *The Engineer* 'An entertainment on the old themes of life, women, fate, dreams, the working class, secret agents, love and death'. This somewhat immodest, pop-art-tinted subtitle is an apt description of the novel. It is work of contagious vitality which even in its most melancholy sections never ceases to celebrate the magic of human existence. This work reveals most fully the essential, sometimes disguised, attributes of the author: his eternal optimism and his trust in middle-class values. In its uninhibited, extrovert, almost arrogant, narrative abandon, the work has few rivals in modern fiction.

8 Scherzo Capriccioso

Scherzo Capriccioso (1980) goes beyond the autobiographical and the topical, which had previously been the fountainhead of most of Škvorecký's novels and short stories. The 600-page novel constitutes a fictionalised 'life and times' of the Czech composer, Antonín Dvořák. Despite his use of extensive biographical source material, generously listed at the end of the work, Škvorecký did not intend to give an accurate account of events, nor to use the form of the novel merely to bridge information gaps. The composer is for Škvorecký an object of great admiration, to be sure, but this does not mean that he feels obliged to report on every incident in his life that has been documented. Rather, Dvořák's personality is the author's point of departure for a flight into the world of the imagination, albeit a controlled flight. The novel, while containing some ostensibly apocryphal elements, does not deliberately distort Dvořák's life or his art. Škvorecký's role is more that of a freewheeling interpreter. The subtitle, 'A Joyous Dream about Dvořák', might be found a somewhat misleading characterisation of the novel. The dream is of a 'realistic' kind: no surreal implications should be read into the subtitle.

The title of the English translation (published in 1987) has been altered to *Dvořák in Love*. Although the translator probably wanted to allude more to Dvořák's love of music than to the women in his life, the renaming tends to trivialise the novel. It also removes some important connotations of the original title which Škvorecký derived from a Dvořák composition, one of the composer's brief masterpieces, written in 1883. Škvorecký's probable intention was to allude by this title to the composer's personality as well as to the novel's tone and structure. This Dvořák composition is referred to in several places in the novel, the most important references being the following two:

> The bewitching modulation of the waltz, dancing between harmonies that dissolve into G major. Scherzo capriccioso. Weber's baby. But what a baby. A gorbelly. A rambunctious, energy-filled Gargantua, showering dymanic punches, harmonic puns, and little surprises in timbre. There are moments when one's soul is carried away by joyful bliss, only to plunge back into the helplessness of its

own uncertain little roads that lead to the mystery on which even well-trained fingers may get lost.[1] (p. 15) Funny music, but at the same time sacred. Perhaps there is something of the false Messiah in it, the one who moved with ease among lawgivers and prostitutes, rabbis and publicans. (p. 24)

The manysidedness of the little piece represents for Škvorecký not only Dvořák's work in general, but also the composer's personality – joyous but spiritual, robust but subtle, straightforward but complex, earthy but mysterious. To a reader familiar with Škvorecký's work, the marriage of antinomies is one of life's great virtues. He repeatedly celebrates ideas and people who managed the fusion of opposites. Furthermore, the special nature of the subject also appears to justify for him the structural design of the novel. He strives at a form woven together from heterogeneous elements. Škvorecký wants to invent but not disinform, praise but not monumentalise; he intends to entertain as well as enlighten, and to encompass both the significant and the trivial. However, it must be said that the result is not quite up to the design. *Scherzo* does not belong among the most felicitous works of Škvorecký, although, as is true of every work of this author, it has its brilliant moments.

Škvorecký's structural conception is reflected in a deliberate dismemberment of familiar narrative modes. Much of this method has been used by him before. Once again, we have the absence of unified plot and of linear chronology. Episodes are recounted in straight narrative passages, flashbacks, flash-forwards, and in narratives-within-narratives. But while in the previous novels there were still identifiable narrative movements, here the episodes hang in an impressionist or even pointilliste gallery before the reader. *Scherzo* goes well beyond the formlessness of his previous work. This results from the fact that the important unifying feature of the quasi-autobiographical novels, the first-person narrative point of view, is not used in this work. The bulk of the novel is related by an omniscient narrator. Within the general structural framework, there are numerous first-person narratives by individual characters (though none by Dvořák himself), and these are among the liveliest parts of the novel. We have examples of others of Škvorecký's familiar devices – intersecting time planes, the fragmentisation of narrative strands, stylised epistolary passages, and so forth. A new feature is the accentuation of the shifting narrative levels by the employment of different fonts (not used in the English translation).

Dvořák was born in 1841 and died in 1904. However, the novel stretches over a period from about 1865 to the 1940s. This unusual feature is because part of what is learned about Dvořák is not through direct action but through the reminiscences of those who knew him personally. These reminiscences, many of which take place after his death, take the form of tales based on memory, of correspondence, or of interior monologues. In spite of the long time span, the account of Dvořák's life is extremely idiosyncratic. With the exception of the description of his family life and his relationship with the Čermáks, there is little about his private life. His career as a musician prior to the 1880s – including his important activities outside Bohemia – is almost ignored. The high point of the novel is Dvořák's visit to the United States in early 1880, when he taught at the New York Conservatory. In view of the fact that Dvořák's stay in the New World lasted only two years, anybody who reads the novel for a balanced picture of the composer will be disappointed. The emphasis on Dvořák's brief New World career has to be viewed as a personal statement by Škvorecký. The basically affectionate, albeit sometimes contradictory, assessment of Dvořák and his family's experience mirrors the author's own problems with assimilation in the New World. In this as well as in some other respects, Dvořák is a kindred spirit for Škvorecký. In comparison with *Miracle* and *The Engineer*, Škvorecký's assessment of America in this novel is benevolent.

The work consists of twenty-six chapters, whose lengths vary widely. The longest is forty-six pages and the shortest a mere fourteen. Each chapter is headed by a brief title that outlines its content, although, because of the author's method of intertwining themes and time levels, usually only one aspect of the chapter is indicated in its title. Alongside the titles, the chapters are also prefaced by a photograph of a character who plays a significant (but not necessarily the major) role in the chapter. Many of the pictures are of the composer at various stages of his life, or of members of his family. However, the chapter titles and the photographs refer also to a large number of Dvořák's contemporaries: composers, musicians, critics, intimate and casual acquaintances, and benefactors. Some of them are well known, others are of minor historical importance, but are raised to prominence by Škvorecký for one reason or another.

Love stories, serious and comic, occupy a significant place in Škvorecký's fiction in general, and *Scherzo* does not entirely depart from this pattern. Obviously enough, the author was to a large extent restricted by known facts and he did not make any bold excursions into the utterly unknown with respect to the composer or the other characters. Nevertheless, an important part of the novel is constituted by three love triangles. The first includes Dvořák and the two Čermák sisters, Josephine and Anna; the second, Josephine's vacillations in deciding between Dvořák and Count Kounic; the third is a replica of the second, showing the indecision of Otylie, Dvořák's eldest daughter, towards her two suitors, J. J. Kovařík, an American of Czech extraction, and Josef Suk, Dvořák's disciple and secretary, later a successful composer himself.

The first two triangles, which may also be regarded as a quadrangle that includes Dvořák, Josephine and Anna Čermák, and Count Kounic, are developed in several chapters of the novel in a random chronological sequence. In 1865, when he was only twenty-four years old, Dvořák was employed as the Čermák sisters' music teacher. Their father, a prosperous Prague goldsmith, was a man of high culture, and the musical education of his daughters went well beyond customary standards. Josephine, his eldest daughter, eventually became an actress, and Anna a singer. Josephine was a delicate and sickly woman to whom Dvořák was immediately attracted. Allegedly, he proposed to her but was rejected. Josephine, however, never entirely dismissed his courting, while at the same time encouraging Count Kounic. After some eight years, the situation became more complicated by her seven-years-younger sister winning progressively more and more of Dvořák's attention. The two eventually married, but it is not clear whether this was because of Anna's unwanted pregnancy or Dvořák's unreserved preference. Josephine did not marry Kounic until 1877, but Dvořák exhibited platonic affection for her right up to her premature death in 1895. Dvořák's own marriage to Anna turned out to be extremely happy.

While Škvorecký highlights, rather than develops, the love stories in several independent scenes, he does not expect a knowledge of Dvořák's life on the part of the reader. A reader used to Škvorecký's sensitive but robust use of amorous situations will find little resemblance between *Scherzo* and his other works. Deprived of a modern, uninhibited ambiance, the author has created self-conscious character groupings and stock situations, reminiscent of nineteenth-century novels, but without their aplomb. The two sisters are conceived of as traditional contrasting types. The older Josephine is beautiful and enigmatic, while Anna is somewhat plain and down-to-earth. Both women manifest an element of mischief in their treatment of their male opposites. There is a healthy jealousy between them, but their mutual affection dominates. Dvořák is cast into the role of a somewhat clumsy, but still engaging, provincial, who is not fully aware of his masculine appeal. Anna refers to him, affectionately, as nincompoop ('nekňuba'). Count Kounic is a dignified gentleman, but he too is awkward in his amorous pursuit. The initiatives of the females make things happen. The chapters describing the key scenes leading to betrothals are appropriately called the snaring ('lapení') of the two men, and are narrated in a manner suggestive of the *ars amandi* literary tradition. Psychology is underdeveloped and we never fully understand why Josephine spurned Dvořák, or what caused the considerable delay in her marrying Kounic. Some passages read like a pastiche of a Victorian novel. They do not appear to be ironic; take the following example:

> He waited patiently until she had finished her crocheting so that he could begin the lesson. She finished the row and smoothed out the half-finished table-cover for him to admire.
> He looked at her work without the slightest interest. But she had her plan.
> 'Do you like it?'
> 'Certainly,' he said, gloomily; the tone of his voice showed no enthusiasm.
> 'Do you want me to make one like this for you?'
> 'Oh, Miss Annie, you don't have to do that.'
> I know I don't have to, my little Dvořák, she thought to herself and he completed the sentence.
> 'I wouldn't have anywhere to put it. I have only bare essentials in my apartment.'
> 'But you have a pianoforte, don't you?'
> 'Yes, but it is not mine. It belongs to Anger and it is actually a spinet.'
> 'That is the right place for my cover.'
> 'You are awfully kind, Miss Annie, but I can't –'
> 'And I'll even embroider your monograph on it!'
> 'But that –'
> Then she proceeded with her plan; she put the coverlet in her lap and looked into his eyes. (p. 365)

Pallid as they are, the episodes describing Dvořák's relationship with the Čermák sisters do contain at least some lively moments. The story of Otylie and her two suitors, on the other hand, hardly ever rises above the level of a comedy of manners. The author uses structural complexity to hold the reader's attention, such as when he intermingles scenes involving the two males and Otylie, in which it is sometimes not quite clear which of the men, Kovařík or Suk, she is dealing with. But the narrative never goes as far as deliberately to imply a fusion of the two individuals in the sexual subconscious of the teenage girl. On the contrary, the love scenes are on the safe side, describing the relationship as being on a high level of spirituality, with only a few circumlocutory hints at the physical aspect of the man-woman interaction.

There are scenes of endearment, harmless outbursts of jealousy, and predictable parental interference. Dvořák's conduct, particularly, falls within the scope of an old-fashioned, overbearing but warm-hearted pater familias. The treatment is anecdotal, the climax of the conflict being an abortive attempt of the under-age Otylie and Kovařík to elope. The episode has a tongue-in-cheek melodramatic ending: Kovařík arranges for a secret wedding to be performed in a nearby parish. Owing to several circumstances attributable to the priest's disorganised nature, the ceremony is repeatedly delayed. One delay is caused by his having left his Bible at home, where it serves as a replacement for a broken chair leg. When the ceremony eventually does start and the couple are about to exchange vows, the wedding is interrupted by Mrs Dvořák, who, having been tipped off about the elopement, has dashed into the church literally at the last moment.

When the novel was published in English, the reviewer for the *New York Times* commented that Otylie is 'out of a novel for teenagers'.[2] The irony is that, in order to support his point, he erroneously referred to a dialogue not between Otylie and her suitors, but between Anna and Dvořák. The mistake is quite understandable. Some situations in the love stories are so similar that they become interchangeable. The similarity between the male characters is particularly striking. They are all well meaning, honest, but shy and rather excitable, and prone to allowing their female counterparts to dictate the tone of the relationship. To highlight this aspect, the author uses analogous stereotypical physical details to describe their awkward natures and their inability to control their feelings when dealing with women (stuttering, blushing, gulping and so on).

The love scenes involving Dvořák himself are the least successful parts of Škvorecký's portrayal of his personality. When the focus moves outside the love theme, the narrative gains substantially in interest. But Škvorecký's portrayal is tentative in many other situations as well. Dvořák is understood by Škvorecký to have been a man of considerable sensuality, albeit a sensuality that is suppressed by his moral and religious scruples. According to Škvorecký, Jeanette Thurber, the patroness of the arts who was responsible for Dvořák's coming to America, understood this point better than anybody else. To her he was 'deep in his soul, a dandy'. (p. 218) No less explicit in this regard are allusions by the nymph of the novel, the pianist Adèle Margolies. However, there is little evidence of this aspect of Dvořák's character in the novel itself. The premarital sexual relationship between him and Anna is used as a frequent point of reference by various characters. However, the scene describing the consummation of their affair hardly shows a passionate male; Dvořák is to a large degree pushed into sexual intercourse by the innocent but determined young woman. Nor is his having fathered nine children any more convincing a proof of Dvořák's sensuality. After all, he was a devout Catholic, and of peasant stock.

The premarital affair that resulted in Anna's pregnancy comes to burden Dvořák's conscience. The early death of his first three children is regarded by him as an atonement for his sins. However, Škvorecký conceives of Dvořák as a life-affirmative individual, and his guilt feelings do not constitute some chronic neurosis that might permanently cripple his personality. The last thing Škvorecký wanted was to make Dvořák into a morbid individual whose art is nourished by deep-seated internal conflicts. Dvořák is a man who 'sits on two stools. One is in heaven, and the other on earth'. (p. 27) If occasional tension arises from this duality, it is healthy within Škvorecký's conception of Christianity. Dvořák is a man of deep faith, whose conception of religion is influenced by the powerful imagination that accompanies his peasant extraction. 'He believes [in Paradise] literally. It seems to me that he conceives of it as a permanent feast, where there is an abundance of everything for everybody', comments Jeanette Thurber. (pp. 86–7)

Dvořák's dual nature is observed in other aspects of his life as well. He is shown as loving the most ordinary, mundane life-style. He likes his small village in Bohemia, his family milieu, his pigeon coop, and particularly the little pubs which abound in good beer. But he also likes the hustle and bustle of New York. Watching trains and steamboats is one of his favourite pastimes. He indulges in such common entertainments as dumpling-eating contests, but strikes an impressive fire on such formal occasions as when he receives an honorary degree at Cambridge University, or when he attends social functions where he is surrounded by the wealthy patrons of the New World. His family background – his father was a serf – also motivates his social consciousness. He sympathises deeply with the poor and is horrified by some of the scenes he witnesses in the New York slums. His sympathy for the poor and the oppressed also makes him a champion of the blacks. Škvorecký extensively dramatises this quality, seemingly to the point of exaggeration. His depiction of Dvořák's close personal relations with American black musicians contains some apocryphal elements. In financial matters he is impractical; his wife is constantly forced to intervene on his behalf in this area, sometimes to his embarrassment. He becomes easily angry, sometimes without cause, but his anger is usually short-lived. His considerable natural vitality is occasionally uncontrolled. This point is made obvious in the novel, but it is shown as an endearing aspect of Dvořák, rather than deserving of criticism.

Škvorecký's depiction of the composer basically follows the generally accepted paradoxical understanding of Dvořák: a simple man of considerable complexity. It has appropriately been pointed out that Škvorecký's portrayal contains certain elements derived from popular art, like Hollywood movies dealing with famous men. The common device of contrasting the genius's work with his private life is used extensively. For example, Adèle's first visit to Dvořák's home is described by her as follows:

> An unreal feeling. In the midst of the smell of dumplings and the noise of pigeons, the runny nose of his daughter Lojzička and his seeming blindness to the seductive behaviour of his associate towards his innocent daughter, the most unbelievable melodies, which perhaps otherwise only Schubert could produce, the blends of timbre; his heavenly music is born. She looked at this divinely endowed man. He was looking sadly into his beer mug, in which the froth had now settled down, and then he pulled a handkerchief out of his pocket, just like the trombone player earlier, but his Carolingian nose surpassed even the feat of that hapless man. (p. 31)

Dvořák's naïveté in wordly matters, his absentmindedness and preoccupation with trivial things, are shown in a similar vein.

Naturally, Dvořák's music is given a prominent role in the novel. In his youth Škvorecký was a competent amateur musician, and his understanding of music is abundantly reflected in his works. Some of the best passages of the novel consist of descriptions of Dvořák's art;

some are impressionistic, when the author uses simple but effective imagery; some are couched in technical, musicological terms. The narrative method varies widely in the parts dealing with music. There are scenes featuring Dvořák himself as composer, musician, teacher and conductor. There are discussions of his work by his contemporaries, which range from sophisticated (for example, the critic Huneker) to amateurish. There are reminiscences of those who survived him which reach into the 1940s, notably Jeanette who lived into her late 90s. Finally, there are purely anecdotal scenes.

The various accounts are not always consistent. Dvořák's moody treatment of his pupils is developed convincingly, but his art of conducting is filled with contradictions. On the one hand, he is portrayed as a typical tyrannical primadonna, almost to the point of caricature. On the other hand, he is considered by some characters to be insufficiently assertive when dealing with orchestras. The evaluation of Dvořák's art of composing is not without personal bias. Škvorecký essentially discounts the Brahmsian structural element and overemphasises the native folk influence. Brahms is in fact contrasted with Dvořák as a composer of a different kind and claimed to be of a lesser stature. According to Škvorecký's account, the acme of Dvořák's work came during the mid-1880s, with *The New World Symphony* and the *Cello Concerto* receiving, besides *Scherzo Capriccioso*, the greatest attention. The novel treats the dispute over the influence of American folk music on these works rather one-sidedly. According to the novel, *The New World Symphony* is profoundly related to Negro spirituals, and the author uses not only musicological arguments, but also apocryphal incidents to prove his point. Several characters, especially the black singer Harry T. Burleigh, are made crown witnesses to the origin of key controversial passages in *The New World Symphony*. The origins of the largo movement are traced to spirituals Burleigh had acquainted Dvořák with, as well as to stories about his and his ancestors' lives. (It is mostly believed that the work was actually influenced by American literary models.) The use of the cor anglais as a solo instrument in the second movement was allegedly inspired by Burleigh's story about the unusual timbre of his grandfather's voice. Škvorecký in general leans towards the romantic conception of music, stressing more the irrational, personal, and accidental, at the expense of the technical and the methodical. A striking example is the chapter 'The Mystery of the Ending', which revolves around Dvořák's dispute with his friend Hanuš Wihan concerning the inclusion of a cadenza in his *Cello Concerto*. The chapter's interpretation of music as something inscrutably subjective and enigmatic to the point of mysteriousness, derived from the alleged life-long impact of the dispute upon Wihan, draws palpable inspiration from the romantic tradition (as does Škvorecký's novella 'The Bass Saxophone').

Škvorecký's most subjective touch lies in his assertion of Dvořák's affinity with jazz, a music that came into its own only a couple of decades after his death. Dvořák's ex-friends and admirers find a link between Dvořák and Duke Ellington, Johnny Hodges, Harry Cartney, and even Tommy Dorsey. In addition, the music of George Gershwin is believed to be possibly Dvořák-inspired, since he was taught composition by Goldmark, one of Dvořák's favourite disciples during his sojourn in New York.

The anecdotal chapters and scenes in the novel are many and varied. Some are transparent apocrypha about Dvořák, the man and the composer. Unlike the largo episode, which, albeit obviously invented by the author, is intended to be a serious commentary on Dvořák's work, many of the stories are undisguised inventions. One such anecdote, for example, implies that the idea for Dvořák's opera *Rusalka* (The Water Sprite) came from his secretly watching Gloria Vanderbilt bathing in the nude at midnight. A special place is occupied by two chapters featuring a tuba player called the Little Man, as narrator. He narrates various apocryphal stories about Dvořák to a small audience in a New York pub. According to him, the short tuba solo in *The New World Symphony* was in response to the Fat Man's personal request. These chapters are structured in a vein similar to the Green Man stories in *The Engineer*. Their narrative rhythm is studiously ritualised, this time by the ceremonious announcements of the bartender concerning the number of mugs of beer served during the course of his narrative. Some of the anecdotal chapters do not deal with Dvořák at all; they are independent narrative entertainments in their own right that use references to Dvořák merely as a pretext. Typical of this technique is the chapter, 'Miss Rossie to her Sister Marinka'. This chapter is actually a letter from a woman, currently living in Illinois, to her sister in her native Bohemia. She describes her encounter with Dvořák at a fair in Illinois. The comic effect is accomplished by two devices. The first is thematic and reflects the weakness of the woman's intellect, and the second is stylistic. The letter is written in a blend of Czech and English, bastardised to such a degree that it goes beyond the boundaries of the probable. The letter is a stylistic game which can be

Scherzo Capriccioso 95

appreciated only by a reader with a thorough command of both Czech and English. The chapter has antecedents in the extensive correspondence in *The Engineer*, particularly in the letters of Lojza. Škvorecký seemingly intended *Scherzo Capriccioso* to be an exhilarating experience. A serio-comic blend, it was meant to duplicate the spirit of Dvořák's music as the author understands it. It is difficult to determine with any conviction why he not only failed in this objective, but wrote a work that does not quite measure up to his earlier accomplishments in the novel. Is it because the author felt at all times obliged to look over his shoulder to biographical and historical data, and never successfully solved the problem of what to invent, and what merely to retell? Or was it because the improvisational narrative web was much harder to spin around a man of Dvořák's stature, which then reflects the author's lack of liberation from the official reverence for the composer in his native country? Or is it the absence of a central perspective in the *Ich-form* that deprived the novel of a specific tone? No doubt, the casual, ironically irreverent, 'cynical' viewpoint of the narrator in his earlier novels is responsible for much of their effectiveness. Škvorecký did not find an adequate substitute for this device in *Scherzo*. Strangely, the best parts of the work are those where Dvořák does not figure at all, or which feature him as a character only marginally. The work will inevitably be read with the expectation of an insight into the mind, soul, and art of Dvořák, but it offers little of that. Equally unrewarded is the expectation of some insight into Dvořák's times. This might be because we invariably have higher standards of objectivity when reading about a somewhat remote historical period than when reading about a period of which our lives were a part. A comparison between *Scherzo* and *Miracle* or *The Engineer* shows Škvorecký's narrative temperament to be much more at home in the recent than the more distant past.

Part II
Short Works

9 Short Stories

From a natural story-teller like Škvorecký, one would expect a substantial interest in short stories. However, this genre is only modestly represented in his oeuvre. The reason for this comparative lack is easy to explain. The loose structure of his novels allows him a virtually unlimited opportunity for the inclusion of independent narrative segments. There are countless such independent segments scattered throughout his novels, which could be removed from the narrative context without much ill effect and published on their own. Relatively the most extensive use of the short-story form by the author is in his crime fiction, which I discuss separately. I also discuss separately Škvorecký's three novelle, *The Emöke Legend* (*Legenda Emöke*, 1963), 'The Bass Saxophone' (*Bass Saxophon*, 1967), and *The End of a Parish Priest* (*Farářův konec*, 1969). This chapter is limited to the discussion of Škvorecký's remaining short works published under the titles, *The Menorah* (*Sedmiramenný svícen*, 1964), *A Babylonian Tale* (*Babylonský příběh a jiné povídky*, 1967), and *From the Life of High Society* (*Ze života lepší společnosti*, 1965). A collection of all Škvorecký's short stories was published under the title *The Bitter World* (*Hořkej svět*, 1969), and an expanded version of *From the Life of High Society* under the title *From the Life of Czech Society* (*Ze života české společnosti*, 1985).

The Menorah consists of seven independent stories, framed in a story-dialogue between the author's narrative surrogate and his Jewish girlfriend, Rebeka. The setting of the framework appears to be several years after World War II. The structure of the collection and its title are symbolic, since the subject-matter of all narratives is the suffering and destruction of the Jews of the town K. (presumably Kostelec). Rebeka, a survivor of a Nazi concentration camp, describes to the narrator her own wartime experience. Her narrative is interrupted seven times by the narrator's own stories about Kostelec Jews whom he had personally known. Most of the stories feature one Jewish character or one Jewish family, and their developmental pattern is almost identical: the old-time life-style during the pre-Nazi era, followed by the disruptive effect of the war, culminating in the tragic end, either in a concentration camp or in some other form of violent death. The repetition of the pattern produces an almost physical perception of suffering. The stories are set in the familiar milieu of a little town whose inhabitants all know each other, a fact which makes the stories that bit more tragic. The town becomes the microcosm of the entire horror-laden era, when human values are trampled into the dust, and naked power, vulgarity, greed and opportunism triumph.

The author shows the destruction of poor, rich, noble and less-than-noble Jews, individuals as well as entire groups. Especially compelling are the stories which concern Jews whom the narrator knew intimately as a boy, such as his teacher of German, Katz, and the physician Strass. Katz is the epitome of a Jew of modest means: educated, dignified, but unheroic. Škvorecký uses the character as a conduit for the description of the exotically poetic and mysterious life-style of Orthodox Jewry, which had a powerful impact on him when he was a boy. Strass is a prosperous, worldly man, a typical Jewish physician of considerable expertise and unfailing dedication to his profession. He commands such respect in the community as only few do. Yet even this strong man bends under the ever-increasing burden of daily humiliation.

The last story is of a different kind, describing the devastating impact of a jazz concert given by the orchestra of which the narrator was a member. The change in the repertoire, previously approved by the authorities, and the demonstrative behaviour of the players, results in the arrest, deportation and subsequent death of two of its members who are of dubious Aryan pedigree. Those familiar with Škvorecký's lexicon of symbols, which ascribes to jazz the force of supreme elation and fulfilment, will understand especially well the meaning of the tragic outcome of the concert.

The frame story of Rebeka has a harsher tone and a different pattern. It does not depict physical destruction like the other stories, but rather the experience and psychology of a survivor of the Holocaust. In spite of Rebeka's survival, her story is perhaps the grimmest of the cycle. Her incarceration in a concentration camp from an early age has left a lasting imprint on her psyche, and even after the liberation she has not ceased to feel inferior. The story also shows that anti-Semitism did not disappear with the fall of Hitler, and that it could be found among the Czechs as well as Germans. Especially shocking is Rebeka's encounter after the war with former family friends, who had been entrusted with the safe-keeping of some of the family heirlooms before their departure for the concentration camp. From their reaction, it is only too obvious that they had hoped that Rebeka would not return so that they would be able to retain the property. The frame story provides an intermezzo between each of the seven stories. Rebeka's experience serves as a reminder that the war is not just of epic interest, but an event which, given man's callousness, is conceivably repeatable.

Reminiscent of the method of Chekhov, most of the stories contain one or two brief, snapshot-like episodes which mirror in a condensed form the action of the entire story. For example, Rebeka describes how she had accidentally run into her classmate when on her way to the railway depot, from which the local Jews were to be transported to the concentration camp. Anne, with a film magazine in her hand, was hurrying not to be late for her date. Overcome by self-pity and envy, Rebeka had only then become suddenly aware of her fate. In the story about Dr Strass, the narrator describes how, months after his illness (inflammation of bronchial tubes and pneumonia) he started to play the saxophone, although he knew that the illness had left him with a chronic respiratory problem. One day, long after Strass was barred from practising medicine outside the Jewish community, he accidentally meets the doctor in the street. The following scene ensues:

> I said hello to him and I stopped, strangely embarrassed. The doctor smiled, but his smile was restrained as if he were ashamed, and he asked: 'How are you?' 'Fine,' I said and I felt bad for having said 'fine', although it was true – I blushed all over when I realised that the doctor was calling me by my last name, whereas the last time I talked to him, he still called me by my first name, but then I was only an eighth-grader. We remained silent and I did not know what to say. 'What is that you're carrying?' asked the doctor and pointed at the long case with my tenor-saxophone. 'A saxophone,' I said. He looked at me with surprise. 'A saxophone? But –' and he did not finish the sentence. It seemed to me that he was blushing and then I blushed again because I understood why he had not finished the sentence: he knew that he no longer had any right to ask about my health, to inquire how the saxophone was compatible with my ailing lungs because he was a Jew and this was purely my Aryan matter.[1] (p. 30)

In spite of the brevity of the stories (the entire collection is only 120 pages long), the author manages to a remarkable degree to give a sense of the Jewish destiny. No matter how extensively read one is in this type of literature, the book expands one's perception of the Holocaust.

A Babylonian Tale also consists of seven stories. It is unlikely that the number is accidental. Although none of the stories deals in any way with the Jewish question, Škvorecký clearly intended to indicate a sort of continuity with the *Menorah*. The similarity lies in the description of various kinds of human degradation, generally by historico-political circumstances, and the description of the difficulty of communication between people. Five of the stories are based on reminiscences from the narrator's youth, while two of them involve different central characters.

The longest narrative of the collection is the last, 'The Bass Saxophone'. (This story, which Škvorecký later chose to publish separately, is discussed in this study's chapter dealing specifically with Škvorecký's novelle.) However, the inclusion of 'The Bass Saxophone' as a concluding story originally had its structural significance in the collection. The theme of music, around which this novella revolves, is also present in the opening story, 'The Song of Bygone Years'. It is a threnody for the jazz era; now jazz is replaced by rock, which the narrator regards as an inferior musical form. The motif of the decline in interest in jazz by the new generation (Škvorecký was in his forties when he wrote the story) is also utilised for the dramatisation of the lost youth theme. Jazz is a symbol of liberation for Škvorecký, but only seldom is it allowed in his work to run its full course, uninhibited. Škvorecký's wartime stories with the jazz theme repeatedly describe the threatening fist of the Brown Shirt. In the post-war stories, the Communist government plays the same role. When jazz ceases to be persecuted by the Communist ideologues in the 1960s, it is already too late: the interest has in the meantime shifted towards rock while jazz continues to be the passion of the lost generation.

'The Song of Bygone Years' is not merely a mood story. The crippling effect of Stalinism on the lives of young people is shown in the fate of a female singer, whom the narrator meets many years after an incident that destroyed her career. A jazz concert given by a military band, of which the singer was a guest member, offended one high-ranking Communist to such a degree that he demanded her expulsion from the conservatory where she was studying Classical music. When the narrator meets her, she is no longer young, and no longer beautiful. She is a run-of-the-mill entertainer in a night-club, not even allowed to sing jazz songs, which she still loves, this time because of a lack of interest on the part of the customers. She and the narrator, with their love of jazz, are witnesses of a bygone era, comforted only by nostalgic reminiscences of once-popular tunes. The theme of incompatibility and inadvertent abuse is developed with Chekhovian subtlety in the title story, 'The Babylonian Tale'. It is set in post-war Prague when, on occasion, members of the American forces visited the city as tourists. The story brings together a Prague girl of loose morals, with an appetite for sex and foreign goods, and an American officer who had been a college instructor before he was inducted into the army. On one level, the story is an ironical reversal of the clichéd situation, where an uncultured, oversexed American encounters an elegant, sophisticated European woman. This American is more interested in Prague's ancient relics than in sex, and the uneducated and unintelligent but pretty girl is compelled to accompany him through the streets of the Old Town. After a dinner and a dance, activities which correspond more to her conception of fun, she expects to be invited to the officer's hotel room. However, he is overcome by a strangely melancholy mood and deliberately delays the consummation of the affair. He tries to stimulate his sensuality by drinking; the girl is bewildered by the strange conduct of this foreigner.

A similar plotless method is used in the story 'Eve was Naked'. The story is an account of the author's trip to Italy when still a boy, well before the beginning of the war. He is attracted to a little girl whose behaviour contrasts with that of other members of the holiday group. Sensitive, warm-hearted but retiring, the girl does not participate in the group's pranks and escapades. The story's climax is a brief, condensed scene, which reminds us of the technique Škvorecký used in *The Menorah*. One day the group goes for a walk to the beach when the weather becomes unexpectedly pleasant. Most of them go swimming, but the little girl has not taken her bathing suit with her. Claiming that she is too young to be ashamed, the female teacher in charge of the group makes the girl take a swim without a bathing suit. The narrator recollects the shock the event gave him; he saw the teacher's forcing the girl to swim naked as a cruel form of humiliation. 'Suddenly I felt dizzy. And a strange emotion overcame me. And then I felt very sad, so sad that I cannot express it in words. Because I had encountered the misery of life. The misery, because of which death is not indifferent to man'.[2] (p. 38)

From the Life of High Society is of less interest. It consists of the comic diary entries and letters of several individuals from the pre-war era. The diary entries and letters were originally written to be read aloud at a prominent Prague intellectual cabaret.

10 Novelle

Škvorecký is the author of three short works that he himself called novellas: *The Emöke Legend* (*Legenda Emöke*), 'The Bass Saxophone', (*'Bass Saxophon'*), and *The End of a Parish Priest* (*Farářův konec*). *The Emöke Legend* was written in 1958 and published in Czechoslovakia in 1963. The English translation of *Emöke* appeared in a book form in 1977 together with 'The Bass Saxophone' under the title *The Bass Saxophone*. Besides the two novelle, the book contained a preface entitled 'Red Music', in which Škvorecký discussed the impact of jazz on his generation. In both novelle, the motif of jazz recurs, and in the second, the motif is developed into a dominant theme. Although 'The Bass Saxophone' was written in 1965 and published in Czech in a collection of seven short stories entitled *Babylonský příběh a jiné povídky* (The Babylonian tale and other stories, 1967), the English language publication of the two novelle in one volume is fully justified. They are written in a similar style and stand apart from Škvorecký's other fiction. They are both among the most accomplished of Škvorecký's works of the 1960s. They were warmly received in Czechoslovakia, but earned truly enthusiastic critical acclaim only after their publication abroad.

Emöke is narrated in the first person – the *Ich* is an anonymous, world-weary intellectual who describes his one-week stay in a resort several years before. There are some slight autobiographical traits in this character, who is an editor by occupation, resides in Prague and is thirty years old at the time of the action. He characterises himself as follows: '. . . Still single, mixed up in the affair with Margit, a married woman, a guy who didn't believe in anything any more or taken anything very seriously, who knew what the world was all about, life, politics, fame and happiness and everything, who was alone, not from any incapacity but of necessity, quite successful, with a good salary and reasonable health, for whom life held no surprises and with nothing left to learn . . .'[1] (p. 62)

The temporal setting of the story is the early 1950s, a few years after the Communist takeover. The state-run resort, once a glamourous hotel but now the epitome of the country's socialist drabness, is populated by Czech citizens of various backgrounds. Workers, professionals, housewives, young people and old, most of them staying in the resort free or for a nominal fee, taking advantage of the new social order. This motley collection of individuals does not get along very well and generally feels uncomfortable with the environment, which had been the natural habitat of the idle pre-revolutionary rich. Many miss their everyday routine of work and simple pursuits. In order to provide their brief stay in the resort with some sense of purpose the management has structured the vacationers' day with 'collective entertainment'. This is directed by a primitive, unintelligent, and frequently intoxicated man with the pompous title of Desk-officer for Culture. Against this background the narrator unfolds his confessional tale of what he regards as the greatest personal defeat of his life: his inability to respond in a timely fashion to the call of genuine love.

Besides the narrator, the focus of the story is on his roommate, a middle-aged school teacher, and a young woman, half-Slovak and half-Hungarian, whose name is Emöke. The narrator's roommate, in spite of his profession, is a vulgar, half-educated man whose entire existence revolves around amatory pursuits. He is the father of three children, whom he abandoned after he separated from his wife. He is notorious for abusing his position as senior master for the seduction of young female teachers placed in his school by the state education authorities. His topics of conversation, his jokes, and his comments on others are all permeated by the sexual. The narrator, albeit himself leading a lighthearted, almost promiscuous life, is irritated by the teacher's incessantly proclaimed sexual proclivities. Gradually, he develops a passionate hatred of this man, perhaps partly because the teacher is something of a parody, a vulgarised version of himself. 'He was a man entirely in the sway of death, and I swayed under the bleakness of that life of his, more desolate than the life of a mouse or a sparrow, or the caged armadillo at the zoo that just stamps its feet on the steel floor and snorts greedily and rhythmically and then eats and then copulates and snorts and stamps and runs around and sleeps because it's an armadillo, a comical beast that lives an optimal life according to armadillo law.' (p. 38)

Emöke is at the opposite pole, an altogether saintly creature. Her father had been a pro-Axis Populist who after the war was dismissed from his position as postmaster, and his family was thus relegated to a life of poverty. When only an eleventh-grader, Emöke was married off to a rich man in his middle forties. Her husband, impulsive and crude, with frequent fits of debauchery, quickly turned Emöke's life into a living hell. She befriended an old, consumptive gardener who helped her to escape from her everyday exposure to lust into the spiritual realm of mystical, pseudo-religious literature. After the Communist takeover, her husband's property was nationalised and, shortly thereafter, he was killed while trying to escape to Austria. Having developed an aversion to sex, Emöke vowed never to marry again. She settled down with her young daughter in a provincial town, where she became an accountant. Religion became the axis of her entire existence.

The action of the novella revolves around the dynamics of alternating attraction and repulsion that obtains between the narrator and Emöke. Despite her past torment, she is a very good-looking woman, 'built like a dancer, slender as a street lantern, with boyish hips and delicate sloping shoulders, and breasts like the breasts of stylized statues, that did not disturb the slender young symmetry of the jersey-clad body. And almond eyes, gazelle's eyes, dark as a charred core of a charcoal pile, and hair like a Gypsy's but brushed to the flat sheen of black marble'. (p. 39) It did not take long for the narrator, used to trivial relations with easy-going females, to fall in love with the ethereal, unsexed, tough and yet strangely appealing woman, a Madonna and ballerina in one. The narrator's intellectual superiority over her is immediately established. He, a cultured and essentially sensitive man, fully understands Emöke and the reasons for her life-style. An atheist himself, however, he is irritated by her beliefs, which he finds over-simple and without any intellectual foundations. Emöke has and needs no defence against his eloquent diatribes on her religious world-view, diatribes that contain commonplace arguments that dispute God's existence on ontological as well as ethical grounds. Emöke's theodicy is simple but effective: she refuses to accept logic and attributes the narrator's absence of faith to his untamed physicality. Emöke's faith is unassuming and devoid of all pomposity, a feature that has an increasing influence on the narrator. She is clearly fond of the narrator and perhaps even in love with him. Deep in his heart he believes that he would probably be able to seduce her, but his respect for her makes him refrain from using his customary devices. The narrator is attracted to Emöke precisely because of her legendary qualities and possibly believes that her acquiescence might destroy her magical appeal. By the same token, the narrator is a challenge for Emöke which, if overcome, would make her faith rise to heights more glorious than ever before.

The logic of the situation indicates an unhappy outcome, but the narrator's account leads us through a maze of self-deluding complications that range from theological argument to accusations of malicious plotting on the part of the teacher. On the eve of their departure from the resort, it appears that the couple will finally reach a deeper understanding. Under the influence of music and dance, Emöke appears transformed, as if her supressed sensuality had finally began to assert itself, at least in the eyes of the narrator. However, the story's spirit of destruction, the envious teacher, uses the narrator's brief absence to inform Emöke of the narrator's liaison with another woman. She readily uses this information to break up her relationship with the narrator and retreats into her shell. Both she and the narrator make only a feeble attempt, on the evening of her departure, to restore their ties.

The novella has a postscript. The teacher and the narrator depart together on the same train, with some other vacationers. The narrator uses the occasion to humiliate the teacher by exposing his intellectual and emotional vacuity through a guessing game similar to Twenty Questions, where, by means of logical questioning the person who had left the room (in this case the compartment) has to guess the identity of an object the others have all agreed on. The 'object' is the teacher himself, and he fails miserably to find the correct solution.

Graham Greene wrote an enthusiastic comment on the novella, comparing Škvorecký to Chekhov. While the theme of emotional failure, developed with subtle psychology, invites comparison with certain works of Chekhov, and perhaps even more with Turgenev's reminiscences of a melancholy 'superfluous-man', *Emöke* is essentially linked to an altogether different literary tradition. The narrative method, which depends on an elaborate, almost ornate syntax – with a cascading stream of clauses, interpolations, and digressions, running on occasion over a page – was obviously influenced by Faulkner, an author well known to Škvorecký. Indeed, he was engaged in translating Faulkner's work at the time he was working on *Emöke*.

Even more interesting is the novella's relationship to the domestic literary currents of the period. In the late 1950s, in reaction against the pompous, noisy, artificial worship of socialist heroes and grand events, Czech literature turned its attention to the ordinary aspects of life. Led by a group of authors gathered around the literary journal *Květen* (May), Czech literature declared war on Stalinist aesthetics in the form of what came to be called 'the poetry of the everyday'. The intimate, almost banal story of *Emöke* had, at the time of its origin, 1958 (albeit much less at the time of its publication in 1963), a certain polemical character. Not only the plot, but also its elaboration, reflect the spirit of the late 1950s. The simple story is monumentalised, raised to a level of myth, in a manner analogous to that used by such influential leaders of the *Květen* Generation as Šotola and Holub.[2]

The effect is achieved by a number of devices. The story proper is framed by a prologue and an epilogue, in which the universal, timeless significance of events is solemnly proclaimed. Paradoxically, it is their triviality, combined with man's tendency to forget, that gives the events this dimension. The prologue unabashedly employs the ancient tradition of transforming the setting of the events into living monuments. 'But a certain building, a recreation centre – once a hotel maybe, a rural inn or a boarding house – still hides the story of two people and their folly, and perhaps the shades of its characters may still be glimpsed in the social hall or in the ping-pong room, like the materialised images of werewolves in deserted old houses, trapped in the dead thoughts of human beings, unable to leave for a hundred, five hundred, a thousand years, perhaps forever.' (p. 35) In the epilogue, doubt is deliberately cast on the suggestion of the story's timelessness with the paradoxical objective of enhancing its significance through the threat of oblivion. This point is made by the employment of unrestrainedly sentimental rhetorical devices. 'All that is left is a slab, a name. Maybe not even a slab, not even a name. The story is borne for a few more years by another, and then that person then dies too. And other people know nothing, as they never, never, never knew anything. The name is lost. As is the story, the legend. Neither a name nor a memory nor even an empty space is left, nothing. But perhaps somewhere at least an impression is left, at least a trace of the tear, the beauty, the loveliness of the person, the legend, Emöke. I wonder, I wonder, I wonder.' (p. 103)

The method of expanding the meaning of the story beyond its surface interest is not limited to the epilogue and prologue alone, but is applied throughout the narrative. The resort lies in the vicinity of a well-known place of pilgrimage, which gives the narrator the opportunity to indulge in frequent excursions into the realm of myth and folk tradition. A discussion of extinct species leads him, through symbolic associations, into prehistory. The metaphysical confrontations between the narrator and Emöke go well beyond verbal disputes. They move from the abstract level to the innermost life of the characters, and from there into broad symbolic planes. Elaborate imagery concerning events and characters can be found everywhere. The armadillo simile in reference to the teacher is only one of the many similes and metaphors from the animal world used in the narrative. The vulnerability of Emöke is repeatedly expressed in the image of a little forest animal, 'afraid of losing that one certainty of forest freedom'. (p. 58) Nearly every aspect of the characters' personalities is put into a social and historical context through similes and analogies. For example, the morally corrupt and uneducated teacher is contrasted, in a fairly long digression, with the Czech schoolmasters of past centuries, who were missionaries of enlightenment in the distant provinces of Bohemia and Moravia.

André Brink, in his excellent, albeit somewhat far-fetched, article, has pointed out that this particular feature affects not only the overall structure of the work, but also its very style.[3] The typical statement of the novel has a triadic design. A motif is expanded by associated motifs in the form of interpolations and then restated. Sentence structure frequently exhibits the following pattern: (1) mundane, trivial, sordid; (2) extraordinary, legendary, enchanted; (3) drably factual like the original statement. The story may also be read as an extended metonymy of much broader realities: it has numerous thematic and narrative links to World War II, to contemporary Europe, to the United States (through the jazz motif), and finally to the timeless and universal.

The ending of *Emöke* may be interpreted symbolically, the guessing game representing the search for identity that applies not merely to the teacher, but to all characters in the novella. However, to be fully effective this episode would have to work well on the literal level, which is not quite the case. It is over-long and tends to lead the reader to false conclusions. The focus shifts from the narrator to the schoolteacher, and on the psychological level it is not sufficiently clear whether the narrator's finger-pointing at this corrupt man is justified or whether it is rather his unconscious desire to divert attention from his own guilt and failing. This part is also written in a significantly different, simpler style, and the tone shifts from the elegiac to the almost satirical. However, these inconsistencies are barely noticeable thanks to the rapid, breathless development of this work which was, according to Škvorecký, composed in just a few days. In general, *Emöke* has a much more serious tone than any other work of his. Especially the question of belief versus unbelief is treated in the story much more seriously than elsewhere in Škvorecký's works.

'The Bass Saxophone' is written in a style similar to that used in *Emöke*. While the sentences are shorter and less ornate, the verbal intensity is still greater throughout the narrative. Thematically the work has a richer texture than *Emöke*. The nameless narrator is a jazz-struck eighteen-year-old, the author's surrogate, in several respects resembling Danny, the hero of Škvorecký's earlier novels. He describes an experience he went through during World War II, when for one night he was a stand-in for a sick musician in a German touring dance band. However, the actual time is the 1960s and there are several references to contemporary life. Nothing important happens externally and the narrative depends for its effect on rich imagery and the inner emotional and intellectual vibrations (not to be confused with psychology) of the protagonist. The method of monumentalisation is taken almost to its outer limits. Time is virtually suspended. During the individual action points, lengthy passages are interpolated which disrupt the narrative flow. They contain reminiscences, speculations and other digressions that pass through the narrator's mind. The work blends concrete detail with an hallucinatory, dream-like atmosphere that made some reviewers compare the work with Kafka, and others with García Márquez. But what 'The Bass Saxophone' brings most to mind is early and mid-nineteenth-century Romantic story-telling. One can find in the novella the dominant motifs of that period that are here associated with the theme of music: ecstasy, dream, mystery, destruction and madness. Of Romantic provenance also is the conception of art as a tragic struggle with society, with one's self, and with the very laws and limitations of art itself.

The opening of the narrative has a Hoffmannesque mood. It is twilight, 'honey and blood', (p. 107) and the narrator is standing on the square dominated by the silhouette of a hotel built in *fin-de-siècle* style. He notices a very old man in a shabby jacket, stepping out from a grey-coloured mini-bus. The description of the man consists in an accumulation of details that acquire, by virtue of the elaborate, broadly developed metaphors, a decidedly nightmarish touch. His scalp is 'crumpled like the shell of a boiled egg that had burst; one eye sat lower than the other, almost down on his cheek. (p. 111) Their gaze was 'as if in some horrific fairy tale'. (p. 115) When he moved, his bones produced a 'creaking, cracking sound as if every move meant a crumbling, a breaking of his skeleton shattered to little tiny bonelets by some kind of dumdum . . .' (p. 111) The focus then shifts to the strange-looking heavy object that he carries in a case. He stumbles and the case opens: it contains a bass saxophone which the narrator, an alto saxophonist, immediately identifies as such, although he had never seen one before. The bass saxophone, he knows, is the dinosaur of wind-instruments. Difficult to play, its production had been discontinued before he was born. The bass saxophone is deemed unsuitable for jazz, the only musical form the narrator practises, although he had read about a Chicagoan by the name of Adrian Rollini who had allegedly used it in jazz. Nevertheless, he is attracted to the instrument as spellbound. The saxophone itself draws a nightmarish association through the narrative; its case is compared with a 'coffin' (p. 116), and the instrument itself with the 'Tower of Babel' (p. 120); it is 'the fantasy of some crazy mixed-up inventor' (p. 120), 'neck of a silvery water monster' (p. 171), a 'gallows' (p. 178), and so forth.

Around this simple situation, which is raised to the hallucinatory level principally by complex imagery, Škvorecký begins to weave a network of historical, political, ethical and philosophical motifs by virtue of which the story is monumentalised to a far greater degree than *Emöke*. Broad existential issues are implied. Reminders that this is wartime are all-pervasive. The scene on the town square is framed by references to the horrors, physical and mental, of contemporary carnage. An important variant of the motif is the hostility between the Czechs and the Germans. When the strange old man, who obviously does not speak Czech, responds in German to the narrator's query about the saxophone, his first impulse is to cease talking to him, since during the war it was regarded as unpatriotic to talk to Germans. The eyes of two Czech superpatriots observing him during this scene exercise a powerful influence. Through an association he also recalls the imbecile, and sometimes particularly nasty, persecution of jazz by the Germans, led by the local bully, Horst Hermann Kühl. Prompted by patriotic considerations, Danny even refuses to accompany the old man to a hotel when he is asked to carry the heavy instrument for him. Only the intervention of a German officer with a face 'like Nosferatu gazing out of his lemony grave' (p. 116) makes him obey the request.

As it turns out, the old man belongs to a German touring dance septet, which calls itself 'Lothar Kinze mit seinem Unterhaltungsorchester'. He meets them in the hotel one by one, 'a procession of spectres'. (p. 131) The mixture of the factual and the grotesque continues to prevail. Most of the musicians appear to have been assembled from incongruous constituent parts. The bass saxophone player himself is a comatose man who lies motionless on his bed, his lungs emitting a slight murmur. Maybe he is dead drunk, but perhaps he is paralysed by something else. The band leader, a violinist, is 'a haggard little fat [sic] man with a flushed bald head and bags under his eyes'. (p. 130) His head, scorched perhaps by a firebomb, is 'red as a baboon's bottom'. (p. 182) The piano player is a woman – 'grey, curly-haired, two blue eyes, and a big bulbous nose – a clown's face, a living caricature of a woman's face on a bloated woman's body'. (p. 145) The trumpet player is 'an even more unbelievable figure, almost a midget – no, not almost, he was a midget, he came up to my waist'. (p. 131) The midget, however, has an imposing Caesar head. For the rest of the narrative, he is usually referred to as a 'Caesar cut down to size'. The remaining members of the band are a blind hunchback with dark glasses on his nose, who plays the drums; a giant, with only one eye and an artificial leg, who plays the accordion; for contrast, there is one normal-looking human being, the female vocalist with blonde hair like a Swede's. But her voice is fatally cracked. It sounds as 'full of static as an old gramophone record'. (p. 194)

This unbelievable assembly of freaks, 'a persiflage of a Disney film, not Lothar Kinze but *Snow White and the Seven Dwarfs*' (p. 139), has lured the narrator into the hotel for a definite purpose. They want him to substitute for the comatose man in a concert for the local Germans. While the appearance of the group is frighteningly grotesque, their behaviour is very different. They are all 'normal', warm and jovial people eager to please the young man, who only gradually realises what role he is to assume. As it turns out, they all have their own sad personal stories, which they are anxious to relate to him. They are all in one way or another outcasts, dregs of Nazi-dominated society. Each of them was, for some physical or other personal defect, held unsuitable to be part of the war machine. None of them (with the exception of the comatose bass saxophonist) is a true professional musician. Circumstances have pushed each of them into an occupation for which they were not quite fitted.

The rehearsal and subsequent concert form the climax of the novella. The narrator has to put on a Groucho Marx-like moustache so that he is not recognised by the audience. The freakish band looks even more freakish in the limelight. Their music turns out to be of the most debased kind: current hits, schmalz and oompah, played incompetently with a mechanical monotony reminiscent of an amusement park orchestrion. After some initial difficulties at the rehearsal, the narrator is capable of taming the instrument, which he had never played before. He is amazed and moved by the sad, melancholic tone the bass saxophone produces. The number which he plays is hardly music at all, more a primitive burlesque; it was originally entitled *The Bear*, and retitled for unclear reasons *The Elephant*. Nevertheless, he is thrilled by the experience, and this feeling continues even when he later alternates this instrument with his own alto sax. In the middle of the concert, however, he is replaced by the comatose man, who rises from his bed (his grave?), as if by a miracle, on hearing the sound of the orchestra. The evening ends badly for the protagonist – his disguise is uncovered by the Nazi Kühl, who unceremoniously commands him to leave. As he returns to the hotel room of the comatose man to pick up his clothes, he notices spots of blood in various places. Their origin is never explained. From that day on the memory of the concert haunts him wherever he goes.

'The Bass Saxophone' is the only work by Škvorecký that cannot be read simply as a realistic story. It is filled with signposts that more or less force the reader to search for symbolic connotations. The symbolism is many-layered and ambiguous, and some motifs were probably planted in the story just to make it more enigmatic. On the most obvious symbolic level 'The Bass Saxophone' is a story about dream-fulfilment leading to self-discovery and a superior moral awareness. The narrator's musical dream-world had consisted of the glamorous names such as Ellington, Basie, Lunceford and Webb, as well as some prominent Czech jazz bands. Kinze's band is the opposite of his dreams – an incompetent, half-amateurish collection of freaks, whose music contains only small drops of real jazz. Yet it is precisely in this environment that he begins to understand the true meaning of music, a meaning that transcends virtuosity and glamour and penetrates the ethical sphere. Re-reading the narcissistic passages from *The Cowards*, in which music is viewed from a much narrower, almost childish perspective, one sees the contrast with the novella, in which music is elevated to a metaphor of life in general. The bandstand in the provincial town represents a *theatrum mundi*. In Škvorecký's typical unity of opposites, the crude leads to the understanding of the sublime, and vice versa.

Another idea of the novella appears to be that music is a powerful humanising medium that bridges ideological differences like nationalism and racial prejudice. After the concert, the narrator feels that, for as long as he lives, he will be a part of the Kinze band, which has become for him the symbol not only of suffering humanity, but also of universal understanding and almost mystical unity. It is not accidental that during the concert the faces of even the most brutal local Nazis show kindness and feeling. However, one should not overlook the ambiguity of the situation. The ecstatic state of all present is achieved by the trite sentimentality of the music and its performers, and that state of bliss is of a rather base kind: Kühl's and the other Nazis' arrogant demeanour disappears from their faces, but it is replaced by a 'weary craving for some Bavarian or Prussian town, for *Lederhosen* . . .' (p. 175) 'The more dreadful it all was, the sweeter it sounded to the ear of his [Kühl's] soul (or whatever it was he possessed).' (p. 176)

Of key importance for the understanding of the novella is the sudden appearance of the mysterious comatose, and perhaps insane, man who enters the stage in the middle of the concert and replaces the narrator. The playing of the bass saxophonist is strikingly different from that of the rest of the band: it is not sentimental, it does not soothe the nerves or conscience; rather it is provocative and hurts:

> Like a dancing male gorilla, like a hairy bird of legend slowly beating its black wings, the voice of the broad metal throat screamed the bound strength of bamboo vocal chords, the tone of the bass saxophone, not in three-quarter time but beyond it, in four heavy beats through which it slid with an immense, secret yet emotive strength, in septolets, in a beat that went not only against the automatic oompahpah but also against the four intended accents as if it were shaking off not only all the laws of music but also the cramping weight of something even more immense; a polyrhythmical phoenix, black, ominous, tragic, rising to the red sun of that evening from some horrible moment, from all fearful days, the Adrian Rollini of that child's dream come true, personified, struggling – yes! (pp. 181–2)

The brutal solo 'succeeded in giving a cry, in shaking *the complacency* of a dark hall somewhere in Europe' (p. 208) (italics mine). It exposed the true value of the mawkish state of Kühl and his entourage. Hearing its melody, his 'Bavarian dream evaporated like ether, and the softened features began quickly and obviously to realign themselves into the long mask of the Roman conquistador'. (p. 182) In contrast to that, the 'faces in the band glowed with incandescent joy'. (p. 205) The bass saxophone leads to the understanding of true art, which is not necessarily in opposition to sentimentality but transcends it. Only in the despairing roar, the primordial scream, which in the narrator's vision anticipates the struggle of Charlie Parker with music, with the world and with himself, can the profoundest ideas about life be found. The tragic conception of art as a struggle with society, with one's self, and with the laws and limitations of art itself, is, as I have said, as Romantic as the backdrop of the story, especially if one interprets the bloodstains in the comatose man's room as symbolic of sacrifice and suffering.

The novella is not, however, just a story about the bass saxophonist; his role must be viewed in a broader thematic context. No doubt these two perceptions of music – the sentimental and the tragic – are, to a large degree, contradictory within the narrative framework. The superiority of the bass saxophonist's art is beyond dispute, but is the wave of sentimentality that engulfed the audience to be regarded entirely as a negative phenomenon? An unqualified answer to that question is not possible. The author seemingly did not intend to resolve the contradiction. There is a supralogical balance in the novella's message. The contradiction reflects the inability of the mind to grasp entirely and to explain the effect of art. The concert is to the narrator not a lesson, but a revelation. The truth that appeared to him is incommunicable, and not much more than a fleeting fantasy. The experience is solipsistic, and the narrator doubts that it all happened the way he remembers it, and even whether it happened at all. In one sense the night has alleviated his allienation, by making him feel a part of a collective (the Kinze band, crippled humanity), but in another, perhaps deeper sense, it has increased it, by casting doubt on the sense of human existence *per se*. Be that as it may, in the end it made him a wiser, more mature person:

> But they wouldn't believe it. Not Kostelec. Not even the Kostelec inside me – later I wouldn't believe it myself, or understand it. The unattainable message of music, forever locked behind the seven locks of that talent, will always be no more than this craving to communicate, to understand, to go all the way to the end with them – the end of what? of the world, Heaven, life – possibly of truth. (pp. 183–4)

Symbolic interpretations aside, the work's great achievement lies in the author's magical ability to convey musical experience through words and to take this experience into a higher, mythical realm. In this respect the passages of the story containing descriptions of music and its effect on man's soul are unsurpassed in world literature for their suggestive beauty.

The End of a Parish Priest (*Farářův konec*, 1969) is a much less important novella. It was based on a script for a film of the same title which was produced a year before the publication of the book. The director of the film, Evald Schorm, is credited in the book version as a co-author. *The End* is written in a radically different style from that of Škvorecký's other two novelle. Here his style is laconic, of almost impressionistic simplicity, and perhaps that betrays its origin as a screenplay.

The story involves a small village, a setting quite unique in the work of Škvorecký. It is populated by typical residents of a small village of yesteryear: a priest, a teacher, a blacksmith, a village whore, a hobo, and other folk, young and old. The individuals are types rather than psychologically defined characters, which is emphasised by the author's use of typological names for them, generally derived from their occupations. The principal theme of the work is the conflict between traditional values and the new technological world. This conflict is paralleled by the conflict between the religious world-view and Communist atheism. There is never any doubt where the authors' sympathies lie, but the work tries to avoid overt bias. It is subtitled 'A Fairy Tale', but this subtitle refers more to the playful inventiveness of the plot than to a confrontation between good and evil. There are also scenes in the work which are patently anachronistic, such as the portrayal of a troupe of wandering players, which was hardly likely to have appeared in a Czech village of the 1960s; such troupes belong to much earlier times. These evocative scenes are deliberately contrasted with those portraying a crew of technicians setting up a community tannoy system. There are also television sets and other modern amenities in the village, but its inhabitants' overall way of thinking does not seem generally to be in tune with modern 'achievements'.

The plot is a hybrid of a comedy of mistaken identity and a conflict of ideas. A sexton, in part because of an 'honest' mistake, in part in order to fulfil his dream, becomes for a short period a parish priest. This takes place in a village whose church has fallen into disuse after the death of its priest, when no immediate replacement for him was found by the villagers. The sexton who visits the village is erroneously held to be an ordained cleric and recruited by the small populace. He quickly becomes the idol of the villagers, who are tired of the drabness of Marxist ideology. Contrary to his original intention, he becomes more and more involved in the performance of priestly

Nouvelle 117

duties. He baptises babies, weds couples, and is even willing to administer Extreme Unction. These acts are both sacriligious and illegal, as is clear to the representative of the Communist world-view, the local teacher. Not a bad man really, an idealistic believer in socialist-type progress, he understands that the 'priest' is useful for the morale of the village. However, his ideology forces him to become his adversary. Most of the story consists of episodes involving the ideological tug-of-war between these two individuals. The sexton is generally the more successful in these confrontations, since the villagers can identify with him more readily than with the abstract dogma of the teacher. On the other hand, the teacher enjoys the backing of officialdom. As the two individuals do not essentially dislike each other, the conflict is mostly on the level of comedy, even of farce.

Nonetheless, the comedy leads to a tragic end. By chance, a bishop stops in the village while passing by, and discovers the impostor. However, the last blow comes from the Establishment. In an initially mad-cap scene in which the sexton is attempting to escape arrest, he falls to his death from a cross-beam in the church. His antagonist, the teacher, is one of the most sincere mourners at his funeral. The novella ends with a description of a local soccer match. Life in the village goes on, but impoverished by the demise of one of its last honest fools.

The novella (like the film version) suffers from an inconsistent design. The authors appear not to have decided whether to use the story as a parable, or simply as good-natured fun with a few symbolic overtones.

11 Detective and Mystery Stories

Škvorecký has been a devoted admirer and practitioner of mystery writing for a quarter of a century. He has written original detective stories, translated Hammett and Chandler, and has also written several brief essays on the sub-genre. Elements of crime writing can be found in some of his major works as well, notably in *Miracle* and *The Lion Cub*. But while in these works this element plays a role which is subservient to social, political, psychological and other concerns, in four other works the focus is reversed. These works are *The Mournful Demeanour of Lieutenant Borůvka* (*Smutek poručíka Borůvky*, 1966), *The End of Lieutenant Borůvka* (*Konec poručíka Borůvky*, 1975), *The Return of Lieutenant Borůvka* (*Návrat poručíka Borůvky*, 1980), and *Sins for Father Knox* (*Hříchy pro pátera Knoxe*, 1973). While a detailed discussion of these works is beyond the scope of this book, they nonetheless deserve some attention, as their literary merit goes well beyond that of the run-of-the-mill crime novels.

Crime writing has a meagre tradition in East European countries. According to the rigid norms of Socialist Realism, crimes of passion and crimes of greed were viewed as residual bourgeois behaviour and were given little prominence in publication plans. In order to be published at all during the heyday of Socialist Realism, an author of detective fiction was required to build Marxist ideology into this sub-genre by interpreting events and characters' conduct as reflecting conflicts between present and past sets of moral values. However, when aesthetic rules were relaxed in the 1960s, classical detective stories were allowed to appear, and even some original works with contemporary settings were written.

Crime writing always has been something of an anomaly in Eastern totalitarian regimes. In a democratic society major crimes committed by individuals or by organised groups are the most spectacular forms of violations of the law. In contrast, every citizen in a totalitarian country is aware that the most systematic abuse of the law occurs under cover of secrecy and is perpetuated by the State itself. The wholesale illegalities committed by the State or its representatives under Stalinism and more subtle violations thereafter have been the most significant crimes in socialist countries, which, however, could seldom, if ever, constitute models for literary works. Moreover, in spite of public interest, ordinary citizens' crimes are never given adequate attention by the news media. For these reasons in a totalitarian country the writing and reading of crime fiction create an experience of quite a different kind than the Western reader would have. In the absence of the dramatisation of a crime by the news media, crime fiction represents an escape from the boredom of everyday existence to a greater degree than in Western democracies.

Škvorecký's four detective novels differ considerably in theme and structure. *The Mournful Demeanour* was written while he was still living in Czechoslovakia, and it is largely free of political connotations. *The End*, on the other hand, was written while Škvorecký was living abroad, and part of its theme is the conflict between state power and individual conscience. *The Return*, written several years after Škvorecký's emigration, is somewhat less marked by political concerns than the others and comes closer to being a pure crime novel, in spite of its propagandistic ending. *The Sins* is an unusual work for its author, since it is, essentially, not only free of ideology, but also something like a serious parody of crime novels as a genre.

As the 'autobiographical' novels of Škvorecký have a central character in the narrator Smiřický, so the detective stories have Lieutenant Borůvka (Blueberry). However, as in the major novels, the importance of the main character in the detective stories varies. In the first two works, his mere presence is an integral part of the plot, in a manner similar to that of the famous 'master-sleuth' stories, such as those figuring Holmes or Poirot. In other works, Borůvka's importance as a character is marginal. Borůvka himself is portrayed in the tradition of the ingenious but flawed detective who strikes a somewhat unheroic image. Despite his occasional moodiness, professionally he is a model policeman. Physically, he is hardly attractive – short and pot-bellied, with all the hallmarks of a middle-aged man. Because of his rotund appearance, his colleages have nicknamed him Bubbles (Bublina). He is a henpecked husband and a rather ineffectual father. He is keenly interested in women, but too shy to approach them, even when he is encouraged to do so. In the tradition of master-sleuth stories, the reader is able to recognise the closeness of Borůvka to the solution of a mystery in his appearance. His 'mournful demeanour' usually signals a major breakthrough in a case. His sad appearance has another significance: Borůvka's personality has a decidedly melancholy aspect. All considered, the ingenious man who with ease solves one problem after another is something of a fool, a sad, sentimental clown, lost in the midst of the tumult and turmoil of life. While unquestionably inspired by Anglo-American models, Borůvka is at the same time a specifically Czech character.

The Mournful Demeanour of Lieutenant Borůvka is a collection of twelve case studies from the rich professional experience of the Lieutenant. They vary in length from ten to nearly forty pages. The stories represent a broad spectrum of characters and motives, but the developmental method is basically uniform. With the exception of the final one, all the stories are based on murders. Although they are mostly motivated by passion, there are exceptions. Thus, one story features the murder of an elderly woman by an otherwise proper man who plans through her demise to gain the occupancy of her apartment ('The Horizontal Murder'). The chronic housing shortage in Czechoslovakia makes this story almost believable. The reader is taken into a variety of environments, among which are a small-town home, a luxurious villa, a theatre, a fashion show, a mountaineering expedition, and a high school. Two stories are set in Italy, where Borůvka has gone on vacation with his daughter. In one, he helps to unravel the murder of a society lady in the Alps ('Good Old Dactylopscopy'), and in the other, that of a retired Mafioso in Venice ('The Descending Light').

Škvorecký relates all these stories with the utmost self-assurance: all are convincing in characterisation and setting. The plots vary from the hopelessly tangled to the brilliantly economical and, although the author sometimes relies on the reader's knowledge of esoteric matters, the narrative is rarely monotonous. Most of the stories have their Watson, usually in Borůvka's subordinate, Sergeant Málek. In all his crime writing, Škvorecký's style is superior to that of the average detective story teller. That carries the narrative through even in some of the less tense plots. His characters are portrayed also more vividly than is common in this sub-genre, and they live their own lives rather than being mere ciphers in a mathematical formula. The pattern of the cycle is designed to bring Borůvka more to the foreground as a character, particularly in the final stories. The penultimate story describes an attempt on the life of his female assistant, who is in love with him. The attempted murder is plotted by another woman, who is herself interested in Borůvka, and jealous of her much younger and more attractive rival. The final story is not a murder mystery at all, but an anecdote in which Borůvka narrates to the same female assistant the circumstances leading to his marriage. The story has a comic twist: the girl deduces from his account of events that his wife's premature pregnancy, which had forced their marriage, was caused by another man, though she is too tactful to reveal her observations to him.

The End of Lieutenant Borůvka is a collection of five stories, all of them set in Czechoslovakia shortly after the 1968 Warsaw Pact intervention. Although they are essentially intellectual murder mysteries, they are made more complex thematically by the introduction of a new element: namely the intrusion of high-ranking Party officials into the investigations. For the first time there is mention of the 'other police', this being the secret political police (the Czechoslovak Special Branch), which has the authority to thwart any investigation by the ordinary criminal investigation department, of which Borůvka is a member. Officially this happens in the interests of the State, but in most cases it merely constitutes a cover-up of the misdeeds of high-ranking officials. In two stories, 'Pardon Miss Pešek' and 'The Case of the Red Suspenders', the investigation of a suicide clearly leads to the conclusion that the death had in fact been a carefully planned murder. However, when the identity of the perpetrators surfaces, the case is closed on orders 'from above'. In the first case, it is apparent that the authorities are protecting an important official from a scandal. In the second, the murder was probably sanctioned by – or perhaps even committed by – the secret police themselves. In 'The Ornament in the Grass', the responsibility for the murder of two teenage girls falls on an overzealous Soviet soldier, who is entirely exempt from the jurisdiction of the Czech authorities. However, not all the stories contain political conflict. 'Fredoledo' is basically a conventional murder tale, and in 'Strange Archaeology' logical analysis is superseded by almost mystical intuition.

Lieutenant Borůvka is not made into a hero in the new political circumstances. Under pressure, he even signs a recantation document, both denouncing the Dubček régime for its revisionist tendencies and supporting the Warsaw Pact intervention. However, he attempts to perform his duties in keeping with his conscience. He has to struggle not only against the invisible men in power, but also with his new junior officers, who approach each case from an ideologically tainted standpoint. Sergeant Pudil is a representative of the new, post-invasion breed, and Škvorecký uses his ideologically coloured interpretations of clues as Watson-like follies. The book has a highly melodramatic *Casablanca*-style ending. In the last story, Borůvka is assigned to the investigation of a murder, which eventually leads to the discovery of the planned kidnapping of a six-year-old girl by two individuals who are in the service of her parents who had fled the country after the Warsaw Pact intervention. Borůvka and his squad are ordered to prevent the take-off of a small aeroplane in which the trio plan to escape. However, at the critical moment, Borůvka revolts against his orders and makes sure the plane takes off by holding the other policemen at gunpoint. For this act he is sentenced to fifteen years in prison. In spite of his lot, Borůvka remains a pathetic, rather than a tragic, character.

The stories in *The End of Lieutenant Borůvka* are substantially longer than those in the first collection. This is in part because of the more complicated plots, and in part because of the more broadly developed psychology of the central character, who muses extensively upon the new political conditions. The extensive interpolations of texts from popular music, which provide a lyrical or ironic commentary on the events make for a new feature. Some parts of the collection are intensely, almost dangerously, sentimental. Clearly, the second collection is less felicitous than Škvorecký's first endeavours in crime writing.

The Return of Lieutenant Borůvka (subtitled ironically 'A Reactionary Tale') is the last of the Borůvka cycle. It is written in a distinctly different manner from the previous works of the cycle. Unlike the earlier works, *The Return* does not consist of several stories but is more like a fully-fledged crime novel; it has some 160 pages. Furthermore, instead of employing an omniscient narrator, the author uses the *Ich-form*. The narrator – and in this respect the novel is unique in Škvorecký's work – is not a Czech, but a Canadian by the name of Neil Danby. This narrative *persona* was clearly invented for the purpose of creating a certain ideological distance from the events. Neil is a friend of numerous Czechs, and this fact enables him to observe and evaluate the émigré community without genuinely participating in it, and even allows him to ponder upon the difference in life-styles between the West and the East.

The story's point of departure is the murder of Heather, the narrator's sister. Heather was a nineteen-year-old girl who led a fast life. She indulged in marijuana and alcohol, and her countless undiscriminating love affairs were notorious. The investigation of the murder is taken on by a handful of amateurs and pseudoprofessionals, including Neil, his girlfriend Sheila, a novice private detective, and Harrison, Heather's rejected lover. Borůvka and his daughter Sue (formerly Zuzanka) join the sleuthing only occasionally. The erstwhile lieutenant of the Czechoslovak police had escaped from the prison to which he had been confined after his treacherous conduct (as described in *The End of Lieutenant Borůvka*) and had subsequently emigrated to Canada, where he had become a security guard in a Toronto parking lot. Borůvka, now a withdrawn, almost crushed individual, appears in only a few brief scenes, and although his observations lead to the unravelling of the mystery, he never becomes a major character in the novel. His presence in the plot lacks organic justification, and Škvorecký relies here entirely on the reader's familiarity with Borůvka from the previous two works. The perfunctory motivation for Borůvka's presence in the action makes it probable that his inclusion in the story was only an afterthought.

The plot of the work is extraordinarily convoluted; it follows the pattern of that type of modern mystery story that depends for its effectiveness less on a logical, crossword-puzzle-like structure, and more on a vague but sustained suspense involving changing situations and inexplicable conduct on the part of the various characters involved. In the previous collections, the sleuthing was generally directed towards casting light on past events. In contrast, in *The Return* the nature of the investigation constantly shifts because of new developments, which even include the murder of one of the suspects. Some of the characters are in constant danger of being attacked by the unknown criminal. Because of the extensive social and sexual activities of Heather, the list of suspects is long and includes members of both sexes, and various ages and ethnic backgrounds. After numerous false clues, Lieutenant Borůvka's analytical ability finally leads the investigation in the right direction. It turns out that the murder resulted from a mistaken identity. The target had in fact been Heather's friend, Jiřina McCavish, a former Czechoslovak citizen. The murder was commissioned by a former Gestapo officer turned Soviet spy, who was living in Canada under the assumed name of an Austrian aristocrat. The motive: Jiřina's possession of one of his fingerprints taken during the war by her mother. But there are apparently other reasons that involve East-West relations.

The novel has slightly satirical touches. As in the *Miracle* and *The Engineer*, the targets of the satire are left-wing Canadians, particularly those associated with the academic world. The narrator's girlfriend

Sheila is the very model of a naïve, ideologically confused liberal, who, in her feminist zeal to become equal to men, chose the profession of private eye. She is a sort of Watson in the mystery, but Škvorecký links her bungling largely to her political myopia. Sheila's anti-Americanism and unwillingness to recognise the brutality of the Eastern régimes makes her offhandedly dismiss the analysis of Borůvka, who early in the case suspects political motives. Only at the end does she realise that there is a similarity between Fascism, which she has always despised, and Communism, whose excesses she has tended to interpret as a temporary and necessary evil. The close relationship between these two systems is personified in the history of the Gestapo officer turned pro-Eastern spy and unscrupulous murderer. The political message of the mystery is crude indeed, and not much above the propaganda thriller movies made in Hollywood. Nevertheless, because of the author's technical ability to create suspense in a manner well above the pedestrian monotony typical of most products in this sub-genre, as a tale of mystery *The Return of Lieutenant Borůvka* is clearly a superior crime novel.

Sins for Father Knox is a collection of ten stories, each of them plotted in such a way as to constitute a violation of one of the 'ten commandments' of the theorist of the detective story, Father Knox. Knox was one of the three founders of the British Detection Club. He came to formulate the principles of a good detective story by setting forth a set of prohibitions. Škvorecký spells out these rules in the introduction to the book and then leaves the reader to deduce which of the rules has been ignored or broken in a particular story. The right answer for each story can be found at the end of the book. The usual task of deducing from the narrative the perpetrator of a murder is at the same time retained. Škvorecký thus attempts to double the effort required from a serious reader of detective stories. In practice, the reading of the stories works somewhat differently than was intended by the author. One experiences little difficulty in the identification of a particular 'sin' committed against Knox's rules. However, some of the stories are extremely complex as far as the second task is concerned. One of them goes as far as to require not only simple ingenuity, but also a knowledge of advanced mathematics on the part of the reader ('The Mathematicians from Grizzly Drive').

The collection again uses Lieutenant Borůvka, but only in the first and the last stories. At the same time, it introduces a new central character, Eva Adamová, a nightclub singer. The first story is set in a prison where Eva was confined after she was convicted of murder. Thanks to the efforts of Borůvka, and Eva herself, the case is reopened and the new investigation leads to her exoneration. In part as a result of her success, in the remaining stories she becomes an amateur sleuth, drawn accidentally into various crime situations. Each of the stories has a different setting, and the author eventually leads the reader on a tour through two continents. Eva is employed by a Czechoslovak agency as a touring entertainer. Her professional activity takes her to places in Scandinavia, Italy and the United States. Even the ship on which she crosses the Atlantic becomes the scene of a crime. Eva is a colourful character, a beautiful, intelligent woman, with fairly pragmatic moral ideals, a character no doubt very dear to the author. In a way she is a foil to the principled but somewhat stiff and shy Borůvka. In all but two stories, the author uses a third-person narrator. However, it is precisely in the two stories in which the central character is also the narrator that Škvorecký is at his stylistic best ('Women behind the Steering Wheel', and 'Why so many Shamuses?'). *Sins for Father Knox* will probably displease genuine lovers of detective stories, but a non-expert will find most stories, though perhaps not all of them, a most satisfying read. Škvorecký's crime writing ranks among the highest in Czech language, second in this respect perhaps only to the unique accomplishments of Karel Čapek.

Notes

Chapter 1
1. All quotations from *The Cowards* in the text are by page number, from Josef Škvorecký, *The Cowards*, trans. Jeanne Němcová (Harmondsworth: Penguin, 1970).
2. Josef Škvorecký, *Samožerbuch*. *Autofestschrift* (Toronto: 68 Publishers, 1977), p. 112.
3. George Gibian, 'Škvorecký's *The Cowards* Twenty Years Later' in *World Literature Today* (vol. 54, no. 4), Autumn 1980, pp. 540–3.
4. Quoted from Milan Jungmann, 'O autorovi' in Josef Škvorecký, *Zbabělci* (Prague: Československý spisovatel, 1966), p. 372. Translation is mine.
5. Henry Kučera, 'The Language Dilemma of a Czech Writer', in *World Literature Today*, pp. 577–81.
6. Škvorecký, *Samožerbuch*, p. 108.

Chapter 2
1. All quotations from *The End of the Nylon Era* in the text are by page number from Josef Škvorecký, *Konec nylonového věku* (Prague: Československý spisovatel, 1967). Translations are mine.

Chapter 3
1. All quotations from *The Tank Corps* in the text are by page number from Josef Škvorecký, *Tankový prapor* (Toronto: 68 Publishers, 1971). Translations are mine.

Chapter 4
1. Gleb Žekulin, 'Miss Silver's Past: The Tragedy of an Intellectual', in *World Literature Today*, pp. 547–51.
2. Josef Škvorecký, *Miss Silver's Past*, trans. Peter Kussi (New York: Grove Press, 1974), p. xvi.
3. All quotations from *The Lion Cub* are by page number from Josef Škvorecký, *Lvíče* (Toronto: 68 Publishers, 1974). Translations are mine.

Chapter 5
1. *Samožerbuch*, pp. 267–8.
2. All quotations from *Miracle* are by page numbers from Josef Škvorecký, *Mirákl* (Toronto: 68 Publishers, 1972). Translations are mine.

Notes 127

3. *Samožerbuch*, p. 313.
4. Josef Škvorecký, '20 Years Ago, Naive Czechs Did Themselves In', in *New York Times*, 20 Aug. 1988, I:27:2.

Chapter 7

1. All quotations from *The Engineer* are by volume and page number from Josef Škvorecký, *Příběh inženýra lidských duší* (Toronto: 68 Publishers, 1977). Translations are mine.
2. Eva Hoffman, 'Books of the Times', in *New York Times*, 23 July 1984, III:16.

Chapter 8

1. All quotations from *Scherzo Capriccioso* are by page number from Josef Škvorecký, *Scherzo Capriccioso* (Toronto: 68 Publishers, 1980). Translations are mine.
2. Walter Goodman, 'A Complex Simple Man', in *New York Times*, 31 January 1987, I:15.

Chapter 9

1. All quotations from *The Menorah* are by page number from Josef Škvorecký, *Sedmiramenný svícen* (Prague: Naše vojsko, 1964). Translations are mine.
2. All quotations from *The Babylonian Tales* are by page number from Josef Škvorecký, *Babylonský příběh a jiné povídky* (Prague: Svobodné slovo, 1967). Translations are mine.

Chapter 10

1. All quotations from *The Emöke Legend* and 'The Bass Saxophone' are by page number from Josef Škvorecký, *The Bass Saxophone*, trans. Káča Poláčková-Henley (Toronto: Anson-Cartwright, 1977).
2. See my 'The *Květen* Generation in Perspective', in *Slavic and East European Journal*, (vol. 117, no. 4) Winter 1973, pp. 414–26.
3. André Brink, 'The Girl and the Legend: Josef Škvorecký's "Emöke"', in *World Literature Today*, pp. 552–5.

Selected Bibliography

In the 'Czech editions' section titles are arranged according to the date of their first appearance. (Short English title as used throughout the text follows in parenthesis.) In the 'English translations' and 'Non-Fiction' sections titles are arranged alphabetically.

ŠKVORECKÝ'S WORKS:

I. FICTION

A. CZECH EDITIONS

Zbabělci. (*The Cowards*) 1st edn, Prague: Československý spisovatel, 1958. 375 pp. (3rd edn, 1966 text used in discussion.)
Legenda Emöke. (*Emöke*) 1st edn, Prague: Československý spisovatel, 1963. 71 pp. (Also in *Dvě legendy.* 1st Czech edn., Toronto: 68 Publishers, 1982. 175 pp.)
Sedmiramenný svícen. (*The Menorah*) 1st edn, Prague: Našse vojsko, 1964. 129 pp.
Ze života lepší společnosti: paravanprózy z text-appealu. (*From the Life*) 1st edn., Prague: Mladá fronta, 1965. ca. 100 pp.
Smutek poručíka Borůvky: detektivní pohádka. (*The Mournful*) 1st edn, Prague: Mladá fronta, 1966, 281 pp. (Toronto: 68 Publishers, 1975. 277 pp. text used for discussion.)
Babylónský příběh a jiné povídky. (*Babylonian*) 1st edn, Prague: Svobodné slovo, 1967. 178 pp.
Konec nylonového věku. (*The End of the Nylon*) 1st edn., Prague: Československý spisovatel, 1967. 123 pp.
Farářův konec [with] Evald Schorm. (*The End of a Priest*) 1st edn, Hradec Králové (Königsgratz): Kruh, 1969. 154 pp.
Hořkej svět: povídky z let 1946–1967. (*The Bitter*) 1st edn, Prague: Odeon, 1969. 314 pp.
Lvíče. (*The Lion Cub*) 1st edn., Prague: Československý spisovatel, 1969. 269 pp. (Toronto: 68 Publishers, 1974. 268 pp. text used for discussion.)
Tankový prapor: fragment z doby kultu. (*Tank*) 1st edn., Toronto: 68 Publishers, 1971. 240 pp.
Mirákl. (*Miracle*) 1st edn., Toronto: 68 Publishers, 1972. 2 volumes (295, 283 pp.) (2nd edn., 1978. 575 pp. text used for discussion.)
Hříchy pro pátera Knoxe: detektivní divertimento. (*Sins*) Toronto: 68 Publishers, 1973. 356 pp.
Konec poručíka Borůvky. (*The End of Lieutenant*) 1st edn., Toronto: 68 Publishers, 1975. 259 pp.
Prima sezóna: text o nejdůležitějších věcech života. (*Swell*) Toronto: 68 Publishers, 1975. 261 pp.

Selected Bibliography

Příběh inženýra lidských duší: Entertejnment na stará témata o životě, ženách, osudu, snění, dělnické třídě, fízlech, lásce a smrti. (*The Engineer*) 1st edn., Toronto: 68 Publishers, 1977. 2 volumes (381, 400 pp.).
Scherzo capriccioso: veselý sen o Dvořákovi. (*Scherzo*) Toronto: 68 Publishers, [1980]. 555 pp.
Návrat poručíka Borůvky: reakcionářská detektivka. (*The Return*) 1st edn., Toronto: 68 Publishers, 1981. 166 pp.
Ze života české společnosti. (*From the Life*) Toronto: 68 Publishers, 1985. 300 pp.

B. ENGLISH TRANSLATIONS

The Bass Saxophone: Emöke. 1st Canadian edn. Translated by Káča Poláčkova-Henley. Toronto: Anson-Cartwright, 1977. 186 pp.
The Cowards. Translated by Jeanne Němcová. Harmondsworth and New York: Penguin, 1980. 415 pp.
Dvořák in Love: A Light-Hearted Dream. Translated by Paul Wilson. New York: Knopf, 1987. 322 pp.
The Engineer of Human Souls: An Entertainment on the Old Themes of Life, Women, Fate, Dreams, the Working Class, Secret Agents, Love and Death. Translated by Paul Wilson. New York: Knopf, 1984. 571 pp.
The Lion Cub. See *Miss Silver's Past.* Translated by Peter Kussi. New York: Grove Press, 1974. 297 pp.
The Mournful Demeanour of Lieutenant Borůvka. Translated by Rosemary Kavan and George Theiner. London: Gollancz, 1973. 288 pp.
Scherzo. See *Dvořàk. The Swell Season: A Text on the Most Important Things in Life.* Translated by Paul Wilson. London: Chatto & Windus, 1983. 240 pp.

II. NON-FICTION

All the Bright Young Men and Women: A Personal History of the Czech Cinema. Translated by Michael Schonberg. Toronto: Peter Martin Associates, 1971. 280 pp.
'At Home in Exile – Czech Writers in the West', *Books Abroad*, (v. 50, 1976), pp. 308–13.
Na brigádě [with] Antonín Brousek. Toronto: 68 Publishers, 1979. 317 pp.
Nachrichten aus der CSSR: Dokumentation der Wochenzeitung 'Literární listy' des Tschechoslowakischen Schriftestellerverbandes Prag. Februar-August 1968. Compiled by J. Škvorecký. Translated by Věra Černá et al. Frankfurt am Main: Suhrkamp, 1968. 458 pp.
Nápady čtenáře detektivek. 1st edn. Prague: Československý spisovatel, 1965. 163 pp.
Samožerbuch. 1st edn. Compiled by Zdena Salivarová and Josef Škvorecký. 344 pp. Published tête-bête with *Antinostalicum.* Selected with a commentary by Otto Ulč. Toronto: 68 Publishers, 1977. 102 pp.

Talking' Moscow Blues, edited by Sam Solecki. Toronto: Lester & Orpen Dennys, 1988. 367 pp.
'20 Years Ago, Naive Czechs Did Themselves In', *New York Times*, 20 Aug. 1988. I, 27:2.

SECONDARY LITERATURE

Since Jana Kalish's *Checklist* is near exhaustive, only very few items are included in this selected bibliography.

Benhart, František. 'Josef Škvorecký: Babylónský příběh', *Plamen*, (v. 9, 1967), no. 12, p. 127.
Brušák, Karel. 'Czechoslovak Literature', in *The Soviet Union and Eastern Europe: A Handbook*. New York: Prager, 1970, pp. 548–55.
Chvatík, Květoslav. 'Josef Švejk a Danny Smiřický', *Listy*, (v. 13, 1983), no. 5, pp. 64–8.
Danny. *Bulletin Společnosti Josefa Škvoreckého*. [Prague]: SJS, 1990– . No. 1– .
French, Alfred. *Czech Writers and Politics*. Canberra: Australian National University Press, 1982. 435 pp.
Goodman, Walter. 'A Complex Simple Man', *New York Times*, 31 Jan., 1987, I:15.
Grabowski, Yvonne, 'Publications in Other Languages', *University of Toronto Quarterly*, (v. 47, 1978), no. 4, pp. 494–6.
Hájek, Igor. 'Škvorecký, Josef', in *Encyclopedia of World Literature in the 20th Century*. Rev. edn. New York: Ungar, 1981–4. 4 volumes, (pp. 243–4).
Harkins, William E. 'Škvorecký, Josef', in *Columbia Dictionary of Modern European Literatures*. New York: Columbia University Press, 1980. 895 pp. (p. 749).
Heim, Michael. 'Josef Škvorecký: Hořkej svět', *World Literature Today*, (v. 53, 1979), no. 3, p. 524.
Hofmann, Eva. 'Books of the Times', *New York Times*, 23 July 1984, III:16.
'Josef Škvorecký', in *Modern Slavic Literatures: A Library of Literary Criticism. Volume 2: Bulgarian, Czechoslovak, Polish, Ukrainian, and Yugoslav Literatures*. New York: Ungar, 1976. pp. 192–8.
'Josef Škvorecký: Prima sezóna', *Svědectví*, (v. 13, 1975), no. 50, p. 361.
K., H. 'Josef Škvorecký: Mirákl', *Svědectví*, (v. 12, 1973), no. 46, pp. 360–1.
Kalish, Jana. *Josef Škvorecký: A Checklist*. Toronto: University of Toronto Library, 1986. 232 pp.
Kocourek, Vítězslav. 'Sedm ramen hněvu', *Literární noviny*, 9 May 1964, p. 4.
Korda, Ivan. 'Legenda Emöke aneb zpověď intelektuála', *Svědectví*, (v. 6, 1964), no. 23, pp. 277–82.
Kosková, Helena. 'Bořitel falešných mýtů', in her *Hledání ztracené generace*. Toronto: 68 Publishers, 1987. 368 pp.
Kosková, Helena. 'Poznámky k nové české a slovenské próze', *Svědectví*, (v. 9, 1969), no. 34–6, pp. 322–44.

Selected Bibliography

Kostroun, Karel. 'Potřeba literatury', *Plamen*, (v. 7, 1965), no. 10, pp. 151–4.
Krištof, Václav and Zdena. *Knížka o Josefu Škvoreckém*. [Prague]: Společnost Josefa Škvoreckého, 1990. 60 pp.
Liehm, A. J. 'Magie Škvoreckého a Ripellinova', *Listy*, (v. 9, 1979), no. 1, pp. 45–7.
Mallof, Saul. 'Music and Politics', *The New York Times Books Review*, 14 Jan., 1979, pp. 7, 35.
Mrázková, Věra. 'Česká společnost v díle Josefa Škvoreckého', *Svědectví*, (v. 17, 1983), no. 68, pp. 739–43.
Newman, Peter C. 'Josef Škvorecký', in his *Home Country: People, Places, and Power Politics*. Toronto: McClelland and Stewart, 1973. 244 pp. (pp. 132–4).
Pletánek, Václav. 'The Language and Style of Škvorecký's "The Cowards"', *Canadian Slavonic Papers*, (v. 13, 1981), no. 4, pp. 384–93.
Porter, Robert. 'Josef Škvorecký. Prima sezóna: Text o nejdůležitějších věcech života', *Books Abroad*, (v. 50, 1976), pp. 193–4.
Schubert, Peter Z. 'Josef Škvorecký, Příběh inženýra lidských duší', *World Literature Today*, (v. 52, 1978), no. 4, p. 655.
'Škvorecký, Josef', in *Contemporary Authors*. Detroit: Gale Research Co., 1976. Volume 61–64, pp. 511–12.
'Škvorecký, Josef', in *Slovník českých spisovatelů*. Compiled by Jiří Brabec, et al. Toronto: 68 Publishers, 1982. 537 pp. (pp. 443–7).
Sojka-Orešník, Spytihněv. 'Marné a trapné symboly', *Svědectví*, (v. 13, 1976), no. 52, pp. 677–88.
Solecki, Sam. 'Writing West/Looking East: The Fiction of Josef Škvorecký', *Cross Currents* (1990), no. 9, pp. 163–72.
Suchomel, Milan. 'O potřebě mýtů', *Plamen*, (v. 7, 1965), no. 1, pp. 66–72.
World Literature Today: Homage to Josef Škvorecký, 1980 Neustadt Prize Laureate. Autumn 1980 (v. 54, no. 4) pp. 501–90.
Żekulin, Gleb. 'The Intellectuals' Dilemma: The Hero in the Modern Czech Novel', *Canadian Slavonic Papers*, (v. 14, 1972), no. 4, pp. 634–42.

Index

anecdotal episodes 50, 56, 70, 94
army theme 23–31
autobiographical elements xiv, 24, 33, 52, 63

A Babylonian tale 99, 102–3, 104
Babylonský příběh
 see A Babylonian Tale
'The Bassaxophone' xv, 94, 99, 102, 104, 109–15
The Bitter World 99
Blažek, Vratislav 83
Blběnka
 see Stupe (character)
Blumfeldová (character) 38–9
Borovička (character) 29, 30
Borůvka (character) 119
Bunin, Ivan ix
Burdychová (character) 54–5

Čapek, Karel xiii, 17, 125
college theme 71–3
Comenius ix
Communism and Czech intelligentsia x, 51, 54–5
Communist takeover, 1948 x, 2, 19, 44
confessional passages
 see internal monologues
The Cowards xiii, xiv, xv, 1–18, 19, 24, 28, 33, 43, 60, 63, 65, 68, 113
Czech Writers' Union
 see Writers' Union

Danny Smiřický (character) xiv, 1–2, 4, 6, 7, 9, 10–17, 24, 30, 33, 44–5, 47–8, 51, 60–2, 64, 65, 66–8, 76–8
 in North America 57–8, 63, 64, 70–2
Detection Club 124
detective stories xv, 40–1, 118–24
 see also mystery stories
Dos Passos' influence 19

Dotty
 see Stupe (character)
Dubček, Alexander x
Dubček, Alexander in works 53
Dvořák, Antonín xii, 87, 88–93
Dvořák in Love
 see Scherzo Capriccioso

emigration and writers
 see exile and writers
emigration theme
 see exile theme
Emöke (character) 105–6
The Emöke Legend xv, 99, 104–9
The End of a Parish Priest xv, 99, 104, 116–17
The End of Lieutenant Borůvka 118, 119, 121–2, 123
The End of the Nylon Era 19–22
The Engineer of Human Souls xiii, xv, xiv, 24, 33, 63–84, 87, 123
erotic themes xii, 10, 14, 15, 20, 21, 34–5, 48–9, 60–1, 66–7, 76–7, 87–91, 105, 107
exile and writers ix–xi
exile theme 57, 64, 77–80, 81

Farářův konec
 see The End of A Parish Priest
Fat Man (character) 70, 94
 see also Green Man (character)
Father Doufal (character) 45–6, 49, 53
Father Toufar 53
Faulkner's influence 107
first person narrative xii, xiv, 10, 33, 44, 63, 104, 122
Foxy (character) 48–9, 50, 66
From the Life of Czech Society 99
From the Life of High Society 99, 103

generation conflict theme 7–8, 10

132

Index

German occupation theme 1–2, 3, 8, 60, 64, 65–6, 69, 99, 111–15
Good Soldier Švejk 24
Green Man (character) 70, 94
  see also Fat Man (character)

Hakim (character) 72
Hašek, Jaroslav xiii, 17
Havel, Václav x
Havel, Václav in works 52
Hořkej svět
  see The Bitter World
Hugo, Victor ix

Ich-form
  see first person narrative
internal monologues 10, 11, 15, 20, 21
Inženýr lidských duší
  see The Engineer of Human Souls
Irena (character) 2, 14, 17, 61
Irene Swensson (character) 71, 72, 76–7

Jan (character) 80, 82–3, 84
jazz theme 8–10, 94, 100, 102, 111, 113
Jewish theme 41, 58, 99–101
The Joke 50

Karel Leden (character) 33–5, 36, 39, 41
Kohout, Pavel xi
Kohout, Pavel in works 24, 52, 83
Konec nylonového věku
  see The End of the Nylon Era
Konec poručíka Borůvky
  see The End of Lieutenant Borůvka
Kosinski, Jerzy ix, xi
Kostelec setting 1, 60–2, 64, 65, 68–70, 99, 100
Kundera, Milan xi–xii
Květen (periodical) 107

language 17, 28, 29, 62, 84
lavatorial setting 30, 70
Leden, Karel
  see Karel Leden (character)

the Left theme 57, 72, 123–4
Legenda Emöke
  see The Emöke Legend
Lenka Stříbrná (character) 34–5, 40–1, 42
letters in novels 80–4, 94–5
The Lion Cub xiv, xv, 32–42, 43, 47, 53
Lustig, Arnošt xi
Lojza (character) 80, 82
love theme
  see erotic themes
Lvíče
  see The Lion Cub

Mamet, David 28
May Revolution, 1945 theme 1–6, 7
meditative passages
  see internal monologues
The Menorah 99–101
military life theme
  see army theme
Miracle xiv, xv, 24, 33, 43–59, 63, 64, 87, 123
Mirákl
  see Miracle
Miss Silver's Past
  see The Lion Cub
monologues, internal
  see internal monologues
The Mournful Demeanour of Lieutenant Borůvka 118, 119, 120–1
music theme 85–6, 92–4, 110–15
mystery stories 32, 47, 118–25
  see also detective stories

Nabokov, Vladimir ix
Náchod
  see Kostelec setting
Nad'a (character) 65, 66–8, 76
narrative within narrative
  see structure
National Revolution theme
  see May Revolution, 1945 theme
Návrat poručíka Borůvky
  see The Return of Lieutenant Borůvka

Index

The New World Symphony 93, 94
North America theme 87, 122–4
omniscient author
  see third person narrative
Ovid ix

Pachman, Luděk in works 52
Palach, Jan in works 57
Páral, Vladimír 22
Prague Spring x
Prague Spring theme 43, 47, 51–2, 54, 56, 58–9
Přema (character) 69–70, 80, 81–2
Prima sezóna
  see The Swell Season
Procházka (character) 37–9, 40–1, 55
publishing house theme 36–9

Rebeka (character) 99–101
'Red Music' 104
religion theme 15, 45–6, 48, 49, 106
The Return of Lieutenant Borůvka 118, 119, 122–4

Salivarová, Zdena xiii
satire 6, 19, 24, 32, 36, 38–9, 49, 51
Scherzo Capriccioso xiv, xv, 70, 85–95
Schorm, Evald 116
Sedmiramenný svícen
  see The Menorah
sexuality theme
  see erotic themes
Silver Wind 60
Sins for Father Knox 32, 118, 119, 124–5
Sixty-Eight Publishers xiii
Škvorecký's translating xiii, 107
Smiřický, Danny
  see Danny Smiřický (character)

Smutek poručíka Borůvky
  see The Mournful Demeanor of Lieutenant Borůvka
Socialist Realism 1, 12, 19, 118
Solzhenitsyn, Aleksandr ix, xi
Stalinism and education theme 49–50
Stříbrná, Lenka
  see Lenka Stříbrná (character)
Stříbrný vítr
  see Silver wind
structure xiii, 1–2, 32–3, 43–4, 63, 87
Stupe (character) 79
Svaz českých spisovatelů
  see Writers' Union
The Swell Season xv, 60–2

The Tank Corps xiii, xiv, xv, 23–31
Tankový prapor
  see The Tank Corps
third person narrative 24
Toufar
  see Father Toufar
translations of Škvorecký xii, xiii, xv, 85

Veronika Prst (character) 78–9
Vohnout (character) 54, 55
Vrát'a (character) 80, 82, 83–4

World War II theme 1–2, 65–6
Writers' Union x
Writers' Union theme 53–5

Zbabělci
  see The Cowards
Ze života české společnosti
  see From the Life of Czech Society
Ze života lepší společnosti
  see From the Life of High Society

OHIO UNIVERSITY LIBRARY

Please return this book as soon as you have finished with it. In order to avoid a fine it must be returned by the latest date stamped below.

CF